SEXUAL HEALING IN MARRIAGE

SEXUAL HEALING IN MARRIAGE

CHARLES GALLAGHER S. J.

AND

MARY ROUSSEAU

ELEMENT

Rockport, Massachusetts • Shaftesbury, Dorset

Published in the U.S.A. in 1991 by
Element Inc
42 Broadway, Rockport, MA 01966

Published in Great Britain in 1991 by
Element Books Limited
Longmead, Shaftesbury, Dorset

Designed by Roger Lightfoot
Typeset by Footnote Graphics, Warminster, Wiltshire

Printed and bound in the U.S.A. by
Edwards Brothers Inc.

Library of Congress Catalog Card Number available

British Library Cataloguing in Publication Data
Gallagher, Charles
Sexual healing in marriage.
I. Title   II. Rousseau, Mary
265.5

ISBN 1-85230-274-7

Contents

CHAPTER I
The Top of the Mountain
1

CHAPTER II
Our Bodies Are Not Our Own
17

CHAPTER III
The Rise and Fall of Passion
35

CHAPTER IV
Isn't It A Shame?
55

CHAPTER V
What You Say To A Naked Lady
75

CHAPTER VI
You Never Walk Alone
96

CHAPTER VII
All the World Loves a Lover
116

I

The Top of the Mountain

PEOPLE need something these days to give them hope about married life. We hear about the divorce rate going up. We hear about thousands of Catholic couples seeking annulments, and getting them rather easily. We are frightened, too, by statistics about the increase in births to unwed mothers, and in the prevalence of single-parent families. Some of us wonder if the institution of marriage itself isn't dying out. We who have been happily married for some years even wonder if our own marriages, which seem safe and stable, really are. After all, in the past, when life expectancy was so much lower than it is now, the challenge of living happily as a couple for forty or fifty years was just for a few. Now, the phrase "until death do us part" seems somewhat more ominous. We're fine now, in our thirties. But can it really last another twenty years? Can our marriages not only last, in spite of the trends in our society, but be happy? Can we keep our love alive, and experience its growth, through the years of mid-life and into old age?

In a way, such fears are a good sign. They show that we have rather high hopes. We really did marry in the hope that we would have and hold each other as long as we both should live. That is certainly better than what some couples do these days – make up a "marital contract." What is going on in people's minds when they discuss, and then put into writing, all the conditions on which they will stay together? What kind of hope is there in making plans, even before your wedding, for the possibility of your divorce? What kind of vow is it that includes such points as how will you divide the property that each brings into the marriage if and when you separate? Making an unconditional, permanent commitment may be scary these days. But it is also a sign of hope. It shows that we have a vision, and a dream.

Martin Luther King, Jr., also had a vision and a dream. When he made his famous "I have a dream" speech in Washington, D.C., he said he was no longer afraid to die. He had been "to the top of the mountain." In that trip to the top, he saw what our present life could be transformed into. His vision of a better life, and his hope of reaching it, gave him the courage to go on with his work, even though he knew he might be killed. His ideal was worth working for, and worth dying for. And so, he spoke of "the top of the mountain." That phrase was a deliberate reference to the Transfiguration of Jesus at the top of Mount Tabor. In that Transfiguration, Jesus and His chosen disciples had a vision of the new life that they were working for, too. And that vision gave them hope and courage to go on, ultimately to face death itself.

Married couples have moments of transfiguration, too. These moments can give us hope and courage, even when the picture of marriage in our society is not very pretty. If we learn to recognize these moments, and learn how to make them last, we, too, will have a dream. We will have a dream in which our marriages last until death do us part. But we will have something even better – a real hope for happiness and intimacy, not just stability. In order to enjoy that intimacy, we have to die a kind of death, a death to self. And that death takes just as much courage as Dr. King needed to risk the loss of his physical life. But our moments at the top of the mountain, when we do experience the heights and depths of intimacy, give us a vision of what we hope for. They tell us that sexual intimacy is not just an adolescent fantasy. Like Dr. King's integrated society, sexual healing is a goal, an ideal that we can make real if we go about things in the right way.

Obviously, the sexual healing that we are speaking of is not the kind described in the recent song that was made so popular by Marvin Gaye. The kind of sexual healing that our pop culture dreams about is really just sexual license. It is the freedom to enjoy sexual pleasure without any restraints, moral or otherwise. But the sexual healing that is the theme of this book is something deeper and much more satisfying. Our kind of sexual healing is the cultivation of sexual intimacy as a whole way of life. It is a prophetic life, by which sacramental couples proclaim, in and for the Church, that

God is Love,
And he who
Abides in love
Abides in God
And God in Him. (I John, 4:16)

Precisely how such intimacy is a healing will be explained as we go along.

There is one big difference, though, between our dream and Dr. King's. Sexual intimacy is a sacrament. It is a gift, a divine grace promised by a loving, heavenly Father. And the down payment on it has already been made, when we received the Holy Spirit in our baptism. Racial integration – Dr. King's dream – has to be a grace too. We can't keep the command to love our neighbor as ourselves without grace, without the Spirit who is "the love of God poured forth into our hearts." But the grace of the sacraments, including the sacrament of matrimony, is a very special grace. Let's look, then, at what the dream of sacramental marriage is. What exactly do couples see from the top of their mountain? What does sexual intimacy look like in real life? What is real life, daily life, like when one lives in the aura of passion? The dream that couples dream at the top of their mountain is for something exciting. They see and hope for not just a plodding, dutiful fidelity to each other as the years go by, but total and constant ecstasy. The high point of sexual desire and the closeness that it brings, becomes the model for the rest of their lives together – all day, every day.

"Gee, I'm surprised. I didn't think the Church would put so much emphasis on sex."

It was a college junior speaking, a student in a course on human sexuality. She was reacting to my statement that impotent people cannot be validly married in the Church. The ability to have children is not a requirement. People who are too old, or otherwise sterile, can marry. But the ability to perform sexual intercourse is necessary for a valid marriage. People who are known to be impotent cannot even have a wedding ceremony. Those who have a ceremony and then discover a condition of impotence can, and should, get an annulment. And an annulment is not the breaking of a marriage. It is a declaration that no marriage ever occurred. It could not have occurred because of the impotence. So, sex is important. It creates the intimacy that is necessary for a sacramental marriage. The Church emphasizes it for good reasons.

But sex means different things to different people. The mere physical act of copulating is not what counts as far as sacramental marriage is concerned. All mammals copulate in the same fashion. An erect penis is inserted into a vagina and deposits sperm. But *human* sex means several quite different things, depending on what is going on the minds of the partners. In a recent *Playboy* cartoon, a woman asked her obviously chagrined bed-partner, "Well, would you rather I was in bed with Robert Redford and thinking about you?" One man's tenderness, when it comes to sex, is another man's manipulation, another's selfishness, another's domination, and another's insecurity. Psychologists hear countless stories of women using sex in order to get affection, even in apparently good marriages. And men often use it to shore up their shaky self-esteem. Intimacy, in other words, is not just intercourse.

What is sex, then, in a marriage that is sacramental? Not all marriages are prophetic, even some which are valid in terms of the law of the Church. A sacrament is a symbol, a luminous, eye-catching symbol, of the inner life of God. In the language of an older generation, sacraments are "outward signs of inward grace." That is still a good definition if we understand it rightly. That is, sacraments are not just mechanical, routine formulas spoken in bored or distracted tones by priests and recipients whose minds and hearts are somewhere else. Sacraments never were that. In order to be outward signs of inward grace, sacraments have to be accurate signs. That is, they must first be persons – not impersonal actions, but persons in action. And the actions the persons are in must be accurate reflections, or expressions, of divine grace. To return to the cartoon mentioned above, for sacramental sex, the woman's mind and heart must be fixed on her husband, not on some fantasy lover. And his mind and heart must be fixed on her.

Why is the accuracy of a sacrament important? Because sacraments are not *just* symbols – they are causal symbols. They truly cause what they symbolize. Baptism, for example, really does cleanse. That's why we use water, which is an agent of physical cleansing, to symbolize the spiritual cleansing that happens in the sacrament. Ashes, which symbolize death (as on foreheads on Ash Wednesday) wouldn't work as the symbol of baptism. If a marriage is to be a sacrament, it, too – or rather, they, the couple – must be an accurate symbol of the grace that the sacrament causes. That grace is our share in the passionate, ecstatic love of the three persons of the Trinity – the utter self-abandon of Father, Son and Spirit to each other. A couple symbolize that kind of love (what a friend of mine calls "the loveplay of the Trinity") in their own passionate, ecstatic, loving self-abandon to each other. And so, the moments of peak sexual intimacy are not just an emotional high. Those moments are "top of the mountain" experiences which both symbolize and cause the saving grace of God. In them, grace enters the couple and heals them. They cause grace by symbolizing it, to each other and to the Church.

Another name for grace is a term that mental health professionals use. It is, in fact, their standard for emotional health and maturity – *intimacy*. That is, people who are psychologically healthy are able to enjoy intimate relationships with other people. They communicate openly and honestly, without playing any intimacy-avoiding games. Healthy people are people without pretenses or defenses, who trust and enjoy each other simply for being who they are. Basically, that is what the three persons of the Trinity do, too. And so, since grace is nothing more (nor less) than the presence of divine life in us, we can speak of grace as intimacy, too. It is human intimacy serving as our channel to intimacy with the three divine persons. It is God living in us, and we in Him, as Jesus prayed that we would at the Last Supper. What does that intimacy look like in a sacramental couple?

We could, actually, put it in one word – *passionate*. A couple who are a sacrament are obviously desirous of each other. They radiate sex – sexual desire, sexual excitement, sexual passion, sexual joy. They make love more spontaneously, and probably more frequently, than ordinary couples. They are free of the suspicions that trouble many apparently happy couples. For example, most of us want very much to be sexually attractive, to know that we "turn on" members of the opposite sex. But that desire to be sexy can have a bit of fear mixed with it, too. We can be afraid that we are liked only for our bodies. Then we wonder whether the people who are drawn to us couldn't be attracted just as well to someone else. The fact that a couple is married, perhaps have been for many secure and comfortable years, does not always heal those suspicions. But in the sacramental couple, passion does come to the fore and heal such insecurities.

There are two problems, really, with being loved just for our bodies. One is that those bodies change, sometimes traumatically.

And when physical beauty goes out the window, so does the "love" on which it is based. For example, a woman who has to have breast surgery in order to save her life might be afraid that she will lose her husband's love when she loses her breasts. Such problems are common enough that large hospitals schedule regular counselling programs to help patients deal with them. The other problem with sexual attractiveness is that there are lots of sexy people in the world. And so, even if I don't lose my physical beauty, someone else may come along who has even more. And then, I can be replaced.

But sacramental couples don't have these problems. They are more sexual than ordinary couples. They don't put the damper on passion – quite the reverse. But their passion is the kind that heals fears and suspicions rather than fueling them. Their passion is total. That is, they are free of the false and silly inhibitions that inhibit other couples. Some couples, for example, won't make love in the daytime, or even with the lights on. They may even keep their eyes closed, out of shyness, and avoid talking about their lovemaking. It's not that sacramental couples try to set world records for frequency of intercourse. Their passion is something much deeper, and something much more constant than that. Intercourse is not the point of their life together. It is the other way around: their life together is the point of their lovemaking. The real meaning of sex is the in-depth meaning of their daily life together. And that meaning can be captured in a single world: devotion.

Devotion is a religious term. It usually refers to our attitude toward God. Devotion is worship, and worship is the complete giving over of oneself in complete love and admiration. Sacramental spouses are devoted to each other. Their lovemaking is just the high-point, then, of a deep attitude toward each other that they live out all day, every day. Such people live in a constant state of heightened awareness of each other. They could never be at a party, for example, and be wondering if one or the other has left the room temporarily. They are constantly aware of each other. They are more aware of each other than of anybody else, even when they aren't together. And heightened awareness is also heightened desire, heightened excitement. Their devotion is sexual passion, as a constant state of life. And passion is a desire to please – not a desire to be pleased, but a desire to please. When passionate spouses are aroused for intercourse, their urgency is a response not to their own needs and desires, but to each other's. The key to such sexual intimacy is in that deceptively simple prayer of St. Francis, "Lord, grant that I may not so much seek to be loved as to love."

We're not saying then, that frequent intercourse assures a happy marriage. It is a sign of a happy marriage. But a sacramental marriage is sexual and passionate through and through. Every moment is a moment of passionate self-abandon. True, lovemaking is frequent and uninhibited. But that freedom is rooted in trust, and the trust is rooted in devotion. I trust my husband enough to respond joyously to his sexual overtures because I know he is devoted to my well-being. One day I was telling my teenage son why it is wrong to look at pornographic magazines:

> "It's because of what they do to your mind. A man who fills his mind with those fantasies might find that he can't get them out of his mind when he wants to make love to a woman he respects and cherishes."
> "What do you mean, Mom?"
> "Well, it's very important to a woman to know what's in her man's mind when he's making love to her. I wouldn't like it at all if your Dad had fantasies like the ones in pornographic magazines when he's making love to me."
> "But maybe he does, Mom. How do you really know?"
> "No, he doesn't. I don't know exactly how I know that, but I do."

It's that special way of knowing each other, without knowing exactly how we know, that constitutes trust. And trust is built slowly, over the years, as spouses prove themselves trustworthy over and over again.

One woman whose second marriage was long and happy contrasted it with her failed first marriage precisely on this point. In her first marriage, she had had several affairs. But in her second marriage, she wouldn't dream of doing that.

> "When you have an affair, you begin to lie to your spouse, and you keep one whole segment of your life a secret – an important sexual experience that you do not share with your spouse. Those lies, and that secretiveness, kill off trust, and when trust goes out the window, so does your happiness."

Devotion, then, is the key to sacramental passion. Devoted spouses don't lie to each other, and don't keep whole areas of their lives secret from each other. The give themselves, their whole selves, and nothing but themselves, to each other. They experience a gradual but steady reversal of their deep selfishness. And it is in their sexual activity most of all that each one seeks not so much to be loved as to love. That devotion is a powerful force for the release of passion. For when spouses trust each other, there's no reason to hold back their sexual desire. They don't make trade-offs like, "You give me my pleasure, and I'll give you yours." They don't make flimsy excuses to avoid sex, like "I just don't feel comfortable about it when my mother's visiting." They are not distracted and preoccupied when they embrace – certainly not by fantasy lovers. But not by laundry lists and dental appointments, either. They collapse into each other's arms with the same passionate abandon in which they live the rest of their life together.

I apologized to my husband on one occasion for not being as sexually responsive as I would have liked. I was tense and upset about something that I couldn't identify, and I said, "I'm sorry, love, I like to give you my all every single time."

He held me tenderly, brushed my forehead with his lips, and said, "Don't be silly – you give me your all every moment of every day."

He was exaggerating, of course – or, rather, giving me a lot of credit for good intentions. But I felt very blessed to have him show me such trust. And I saw, more clearly than ever before, the unique and wonderful combination of passion and devotion that constitute the sacramental symbol of matrimony. They are the moments of passionate devotion, and devoted passion, that are the moments of grace. And it is the state of combined passion and devotion that is the state of grace. Such passion reveals the inner life of God, and merges divine life with ours.

The combination of sex and spirituality that makes for a sacramental marriage is no easy trick. It takes a long time – a lifetime, really – of hard work. In fact, the combination of animal and spirit in the make-up of a human being is not easy to live with in any area of life, including married life. Sex has such a power that it easily absorbs all of a person's attention and energy. When that happens, we see people driven by a selfish drive for their own pleasure. And they don't care what price others have to pay for their own satisfaction. Sex without spirituality is gross, wild, inhuman and destructive. The movie *Alfie*, with its theme song, "What's It All About, Alfie?" gives a clear portrait of a man whose whole life was ruled by his desire for the sheer physical pleasure of sex. Alfie rode roughshod over the feelings of every woman he met, and left them all destroyed, in one way or another. But he also destroyed himself. He spent his life wondering "What it's all about," never finding the deeper satisfactions that come from love and a sense of meaning about life.

The spiritual half of this combination is also easier to find in a "pure" state, unsullied by passion and pleasure. People who make that quest – crabbed, authoritarian celibates, for example – try to seek union with God in some direct way, apart from any warm, emotional love for other people. Such people suppress, and repress, their sexual feelings, fearing that those are bad. And in inhibiting their sexuality, they inhibit their other feelings as well. They delude themselves into thinking that they are "too spiritual" to have sexual impulses, needs, desires, or pleasures. But sacramental sexual intimacy is something quite different. It is a blend of sex and spirituality. But more than that – it is the full development of both. Sacramental sex is not some sort of compromise. Couples do not allow themselves a half-hearted sex life and a half-hearted spiritual life. Both sex and spirituality are full-blown, unrestrained, and generously given to the world.

Does our description so far sound like a description of people who are in love? Does it, perhaps, make you, our readers, think of Cliff and Clare Huxtable of The Cosby Show? It should. For that is exactly what a sacramental couple looks like. They are exuberantly and openly in love. They *enjoy* each other, as Clare laughs at Cliff's comic antics in obvious delight. They *admire* each other, as Cliff truly respects Clare as the person that she is. They are openly affectionate with each other, openly sexual in their words and gestures. It is obvious to everyone around them just who is the center of each one's attention, all the time, together and apart. Dr. Bill Cosby, with a Ph.D. in Educational Psychology, is not just a talented comedian. He set out to produce The Cosby Show with a quite deliberate purpose in mind: to portray a married couple who are still in love with each other. And very nearly every line spoken on the show is a revelation of that love. He makes sure the writers and the actors make that clear. Cliff and Clare, and their ongoing romance, are the center of the show.

The Cosby Show very quickly became the Number 1 show on commercial television, and has held that spot for many months. After the wasteland of Three's Company, The Love Boat, the soap operas, and the cops and robbers shows, it is quite a phenomenon to have the American TV public take into their hearts a show that is so frankly sexual, in almost every line. And yet, it displays sex without the cheapness, vulgarity, and even lewdness that has been the trademark of most of commercial television for so long. People seem to be hungry for some reassurance that passion can be the energy of love, of trust, of honesty, and shared life. They seem to be hungry for assurance that people married for many years (the Huxtables have a daughter away at college, a four-year-old, and three other children in between) can still have that special spark between them. There are several wholesome portraits of family life currently popular on commercial TV, such as Family Ties, One Day at a Time, Different Strokes, and Silver Spoons. But none of them puts the focus where it should be, where it is on The Cosby Show: on the sexual intimacy of husband and wife.

The spirituality that makes sexual intimacy sacramental is the devotion by which man and wife totally give themselves over to each other. It is in seeking not so much to be loved as to love that all people find God. Couples find Him together, in their devotion to each other. When they do, they are no longer like everybody else. They are noticed, and noticeable, by the way they look at each other, by the way they touch each other, by the way they speak to each other. Their awareness of each other, their attraction to each other, their devotion to and delight in each other are obvious to all wherever they go. They live in an aura of praise and thanksgiving, reverence and awe, with the easy laughter that comes not from a tense anxiety about life but from the relaxation born of trust. Sexual couples like the Huxtables are not just like everybody else. There is something about them that is different. And that something is devoted passion.

But what about the spirituality that is the other half of sexual intimacy? Sexual desire all by itself does not make a couple intimate. Here, we can see a horrible example in a very popular stage play and movie of several years ago: *Same Time, Next Year*. The couple in that story were married, but not to each other. They met by accident when the man took a week away from his family to do some annual accounting for a friend of his who lived on the opposite coast. The woman travelled alone to the same place each year in order to make a religious retreat. The two met by chance the first time, and had an exuberant sexual romp lasting for several days. Along with their sexual activity (we can hardly call it lovemaking), they hit it off in conversation. They found that they could talk freely to each other about topics they could not discuss with their spouses. They found that they could confide in each other, and keep each other's secrets (including the secret of their affair). After that first accidental meeting, they enjoyed annual trysts for a period of some twenty years. Hence the title – *Same Time, Next Year*. The story is a series of episodes depicting the growth of their adulterous relationship over those years.

The American public found that play, and then the movie version of it, hilarious – thanks partly to the comic talents of Alan Alda and Ellen Burstyn. But I and a woman friend were appalled when we first saw the movie together. Adultery – double adultery – was made hilarious on the premise that, since the spouses of the two were old fuddy-duddies anyway, the lead characters had some sort of right to their pleasures of bed and conversation. (One particularly repulsive episode had the woman showing up pregnant for her annual tryst with her lover; she even went into labor with her husband's baby in her lover's hotel room. She should not have left home at such a time, even for the reason that she pretended to her husband – to make a retreat).

Every time the audience laughed at this movie, my friend and I cringed. When it was over, we discussed our reasons for feeling as we did. Were we a couple of old fuddy-duddies who couldn't take a joke? We don't think so. We can enjoy jokes about adultery, just as we can enjoy jokes about sex in other respects. Every facet of human life has its funny side. But the kind of humor we enjoy comes from people who first perceive the seriousness of human life, and the awe and mystery of sexual love. When such people make jokes, their humor adds to our awe at the mystery of things. But the humor in *Same Time, Next Year* was cheap. The authors, and the stars, seemed to share the tawdry attitude toward sex and marriage that is so prevalent in our society. To this adulterous couple, sex was for sheer physical pleasure – not each other's physical pleasure, even, but each one's own. *Same Time, Next Year* is the story of two people using each other at every turn, just as they used the spouses that each left behind.

Their self-centeredness became clear toward the end of the movie. The man's wife had died, and he asked his paramour of twenty years to leave her husband and marry him. He was quite forthright about his motive: "I don't enjoy living alone." After all, his own enjoyment motivated everything else he did. Why should his proposal of marriage be an exception? But her response matched his for selfishness. She would not break up her marriage, she said, because she was too comfortable in it. Her own comfort took priority over her lover's need for companionship, just as it had taken priority over her love for her husband during the twenty-odd years of adulterous week-ends.

What this couple showed, then, was not the kind of sexual intimacy that is sacramental. They were passionate, all right – if we equate passion with excitement, with the building and then the release of sheer physical tension, in a context of mutual self-seeking. But that kind of passion is a perverse opposite of the passion of the Huxtables. In fact, the conversation of this adulterous couple was not intimate, either. They shared secrets openly, and understood each other better than their spouses understood them. But their conversation, open and honest as it was, kept the two of them in their separate egotistic worlds. It did not join them in any kind of intimacy. They used each other with their tongues and ears just as clearly as they did with their reproductive organs.

In a sacramental marriage, then, passion is rooted in devotion. And devotion is the total dedication of oneself to the well-being of a beloved partner, not a search for one's own pleasure and comfort. So, we are not saying that sex is everything in a sacramental marriage. Rather, we are saying that everything in a sacramental marriage is sexual. And the sexual quality is due to the aura of passionate devotion, and devoted passion, in which the couple do everything they do and say everything they say. Their life is a life of passionate self-abandon, in which "every little movement has a meaning all its own." Every conversation, every look, every touch, every gesture, every embrace is sexual in its tone and its intention. But that sexual character is one of devotion, not one of self-seeking.

But which is more important? If sexual intimacy combines passion with devotion, it cannot be either one of those alone. Selfish passion, like that of the couple in *Same Time, Next Year*, doesn't produce any intimacy at all. What about passionless devotion? Don't we all know a couple, maybe several couples, who are "just so devoted to each other?" We know couples who care about, and care for, each other, who are kind and considerate, deeply attached to each other, and utterly faithful. Yet, they lack any sexual spark. We might even wonder, especially if they have no children, whether they ever have intercourse. One of my friends recently mentioned such a couple. He thought that they had a celibate marriage, like some other couples that we had been discussing. When I reminded him that this particular couple had three children, he said, jokingly, "Well, then, they've done it at least three times!" Some couples seem so lacking in any kind of sexual warmth that we find it hard to picture them making love.

Are those couples sexually intimate? Are they sacramental? Prophetic in the Church?

That question is a little harder to answer, for devotion *is* what binds people to each other. A closeness that is selfish, even when it is polite, pleasant, even passionate, does not really unify people. Such relationships are not intimate at all, but only seem to be. But the case of a dispassionate couple who are devoted is somewhat different. Devotion does produce intimacy, in all kinds of human relationships. The word *intimacy* literally means "a dwelling within." Intimacy is the presence of one person in another, a psychological presence of one in the other's mind and heart. But only love, unselfish love, what we've been calling devotion, allows one person to enter into another. Any loving relationship, then, is intimate, whether it is passionate or not. A mother-child love is intimate, as is a loving association between friends or colleagues, between business partners, between teachers and students, or professional people and their clients. Any time we act out the gospel command to love our neighbor as ourself, we take that neighbor into our mind and heart. And as long as that presence continues, we have one person dwelling within another. We have intimacy.

Suppose, for example, I love one of my students, showing that student the kind of respect, attention, care and concern that a teacher can show a student. That is a kind of devotion. I devote myself to that student's education. When I do that, I take my student into my mind and heart. First, he or she becomes present in me. I may even have that student present in my mind when I don't wish to, as when my concern wakes me up in the middle of the night with a mental picture of that student before me! I will try to enter my student's mind, too, to dwell in the mind of the one I love, which is what I do when I try to see the world from that student's point of view, to know what his ideas and convictions are. I imagine myself in his place, "walk in his mocassins."

This mental indwelling is only part of the story, though. Any person I love also dwells in my heart and affections, and I in his. My mental picturing of the student I love will produce feelings in me that I wouldn't have otherwise. I will feel sad, perhaps, or angry, concerned or joyous, simply because of my love for that particular student. (In fact, I do fear for my ROTC students when I hear of our Marines being killed). Those feelings are also part of a student's presence in me. He lives there as a cause of my feelings. My decision-making will be affected by that presence, too. I will hold certain values dear, make certain decisions and choices – none of which would happen if I did not love that particular student, and have him dwelling in my mind and heart. And along with that presence, I find myself trying to live in his affections, too. When I learn that the person I care for is angry, for example, I don't just observe that anger from the outside. I feel it, too. It becomes my anger. His joy becomes my joy, too – something I actually feel, and don't just observe from the outside. I'm glad when he's glad.

This process of indwelling, in which one person is actually present in another in all these different ways, happens because loving someone is an act of identification. That is, to love is to take someone to be my other self. To love is to decide that another person's welfare is mine, too, that another person's happiness will constitute my happiness. The Sufi mystics have a wonderful proverb about such identification: you cannot call another person your beloved (says the proverb) unless you look at him and say, "Hello, myself." Love, any kind of love, means caring about someone as much as we do about ourselves. Such caring automatically produces the indwelling presence of one person in another that we call intimacy. Intimacy, then, does not require sexual passion. It requires devotion, but not necessarily sexual desire.

Marital intimacy, however, is another story. My husband's presence in my mind and heart is very different from the presence of my student's; when I wake up at night thinking of him, I am stirred by sexual desire. And the same is true when I am preoccupied with him during the day. If I "walk in his mocassins," share his joys, or fear for his safety, I do so with a distinct spark of passion. For intimacy to be sacramental – that is, for an intimate couple to symbolize and cause grace in the special way that the sacrament of matrimony does – passion is an absolute requirement. Marriage is about sex. Sex is what marriage is about. The marriage vows, "to have and to hold," refer to sexual intercourse, sexual desire, and sexual love. A dispassionate couple, then, no matter how devoted and intimate, are not intimate in the specifically sexual way that makes up the sacrament of matrimony. Passion is the heart and soul of marital intimacy. Dispassionate couples may be very holy, of course. So might those plagued with sexual problems which block a free, uninhibited exuberance in their sexual activity. But couples such as these cannot be held up as models, or prophets, of marital intimacy. For a clear and accurate sacramental symbol, passion has to be there. An ardent desire for a complete unity, desire which reaches its high point in sexual intercourse but is a constant aura of their life together, is what marks a couple as sacramental.

The combining of passion with devotion is not just a simple blend, however. A recipe for sexual intimacy cannot just read "add equal amounts of desire and unselfish love, then stir." Rather, sexual intimacy does something very powerful and amazing to people: it reverses the deep self-seeking tendencies that plague us all. Passion is the energy which makes devotion possible. Sexual intimacy begins, indeed, not with the wedding ceremony, but with the experience of falling in love. Every couple's first ascent to the top of the mountain happens when they fall in love. And what they see from that vantage point gives them the courage to face death. Couples don't often face the assassin's bullet, as did Rev. Martin Luther King, Jr. But they face a death that is no less real and no less fearsome. They face the death to self that true devotion requires. St. Paul describes that death in a couple of stark, deceptively simple sentences. He says to his beloved Corinthians (in I Cor 7, 1–4):

> The husband must give his wife what she has a right to expect, and so too the wife to the husband. The wife has no rights over her own body; it is the husband who has them. In the same way, the husband has no rights over his own body; the wife has them. (Jerusalem Bible).

This section of Paul's letter contains answers to direct questions that the Corinthians had sent to him in a previous message. They wondered whether they might suspend their sexual activities in order to pray and prepare for religious festivals. They are asking, then, about sexual intercourse quite explicitly. But sacramental sex is always in the context of an overall daily life of passionate devotion. And so, we can read Paul's words as an indication of the kind of life a sacramental couple ought to live, day in and day out. Intercourse turns into a lie without the aura of passion as its context. What St. Paul says, quite simply, is that husbands and wives no longer belong to themselves, but to each other. They have no rights over their own bodies. Each has rights over the body of the other.

In the Bible, though, the word *body* refers to a person's whole self. We moderns tend to think of ourselves as made up of two parts, body and soul, a material part and a spiritual part. And the person is more the spiritual than the material. But in the Bible, *body* is a perfect synonym for *self* or *person*. We can paraphrase, then: "The wife has no rights over her own self, but the husband has them. And the husband has no rights over his own self, but the wife has them." Paul is speaking of devotion, of the self-giving love which produces intimacy. Spouses no longer belong to themselves, as they once did. They belong to each other totally – amen, no exceptions, no qualifications. Their mutual self-abandon has no limits. Paul's advice about sexual abstinence, then, makes sense: each must freely consent to it, for abstinence means giving up something of one's own – the spouse's body, the spouse's self. Paul's view of marriage makes it a kind of devotion like that of the Sufi mystics. People are not really living in sexual intimacy unless they can honestly look at each other and say, "Hello, myself." What makes such utter self-abandon possible?

What makes it possible is, of course, divine grace. But that grace is channelled in a very special way in the sexual intimacy of couples. It lies in the self-abandon which is fired by sexual desire. Passion is not just one of the ingredients of sexual intimacy, on a par with devotion. Passion is the energy which makes devotion possible. And we see that magic transformation happen every time we see two people fall in love. Lovers show us something that we don't see anywhere else: total belonging to each other. They come to be two in one flesh – not just in their more or less frequent physical closeness, but interiorly. They are joined in mind and in heart. As long as they stay in love, they treat each other as what they are – each other's selves. Remember all the jokes about "my better half"? Those jokes don't come out of thin air. The people we are intimate with are truly part of us. They are our very selves.

QUESTIONS TO DISCUSS TOGETHER AS A COUPLE

1. Name the most spiritual couple you know.
2. Name the most passionate couple you know.
3. Could these two couples ever be one and the same couple? Why or why not?
4. Describe one of your "top of the mountain" experiences. What kind of healing did it lead to?
5. Where in our popular culture (TV, movies, music) do you see portraits of true sexual intimacy?

II

Our Bodies Are Not Our Own

ONE particularly beautiful episode of The Cosby Show opened with Clare asking Cliff what he would do if she were to die. She wanted to know in particular if he would marry again, and, if so, under what conditions. She put one fantasy after another to him, fantasies of women who might be attractive to him. He dismissed each as "not my type." Finally, she asked, "What if you met my exact replica, someone exactly like me in every single detail?" Cliff quickly answered, "I'd take her to bed immediately." "And," Clare asked, "would you still keep my picture on your dresser?" "I wouldn't have to," said her husband, with a smile at once tender and passionate. "I would have *you*." The end-scene of that episode saw Clare and Cliff in a very erotic, wordless scene on the couch, feeding each other an apple. It was evident that Cliff had set up the scene in order to reassure Clare of her loveableness and of his desire for her. It was also, quite obviously, a ritual they had often acted out before.

That episode of the Huxtable romance made a very important point about sexual intimacy: it does not happen overnight. The building of the kind of intimacy that heals, and that becomes sacramental, is an on-going process. True, its beginning may be so fast that it makes us dizzy. The experience of falling in love is often sudden, even explosive. Many couples have said that they knew the first time their eyes met that they were meant for each other. And in that sudden, explosive moment, there certainly can be the desire for total belonging. The passion by which we give our total selves to each other can begin in the twinkling of an eye.

But it cannot end there. Passion and devotion either grow or die. If they are to grow, they have to be cultivated. As one wife put it to me recently, "We learn how to have a sacramental marriage in only one way: we have to fly by the seat of our pants." We learn by doing. Falling in love, and the wedding ceremony which celebrates that, are merely our learner's permit.

As we "fly by the seat of our pants," we gradually learn how to love, how to follow the lead of passion into a more or less constant state of belonging to each other. Such belonging does not come easily. For devotion, and the intimacy that it produces, is a change in our very selves. Becoming truly wedded in passionate devotion is a kind of heart-transplant. And we know how long and complicated those operations are! Jeremiah, in fact, tells us that it takes a life-time. However much time we have, that's how much time it will take. For it is only on the last day (which is the day of our death) that God will take away our hearts of stone and replace them with hearts of flesh. Jeremiah's metaphor is graphic, because our hearts are so important. We read about physical heart transplants in our newspapers. And it is, indeed, amazing that doctors can take a person's heart out of his body and put another one in its place. The procedure is both delicate and violent. And the result – the new heart – requires special care for the rest of the patient's life. The threat of rejection by the immune system is constant.

The transplanting of our spiritual hearts is just as difficult, just as delicate, and just as violent. We have to do violence to our original hearts. We have to totally remove the stony, cold, lifeless attitudes of selfishness. And once the process has begun, the new heart – the heart of flesh that is warm, vibrant and alive – is in a precarious state. It needs constant care and nurture, for the rest of the recipient's life. For we have a spiritual immune system, too – an inborn tendency to reject grace, to put ourselves first. That tendency is a constant threat to our devotion. Married couples know full well, because we learn it very quickly, that the new hearts that beat within us, those we receive when we fall in love, need constant nurture. And passion is that nurture. Passion is the immunity-suppressant drug of sacramental couples. Devotion is so against our ingrained selfishness that we have to wonder if we would ever even begin to love unselfishly without the impetus of sexual desire. Certainly we know that we would not keep it up very long without the energy of passion.

I remember one funny episode, one day. I was writing a check for my neighborhood pharmacist, and absent-mindedly signed it with my maiden name. I had been married, and had been using my husband's name, for eleven years! I thought that that little slip of the pen was an excellent reminder of something deeper. I had not yet completely made that real change in identity, the deep change of heart, that a sacramental marriage requires. I felt like the child in the poster, pleading, "Please be patient with me. God isn't finished with me yet." In fact, God isn't finished with any of us yet. As long as we are alive and conscious – as long as we have even one minute of life ahead of us – we have the possibility of a new moment of passion. And that new passion can have its own special healing force. A spouse's death can bring a closeness that wouldn't, and couldn't, happen in any other way.

A friend of mine, Fran, spoke eloquently of that closeness. It had been seven years since her husband died, and she had continued to meet with "the group." These were a group of about twenty people, singles and couples, who had been meeting weekly for twelve years, and Don, Fran's husband, had been one of them, too. The group would read the Bible together and share their reflections on it, usually with the guidance of a theologian or priest. One evening, I was their invited guest. They had asked me to make a brief presentation on spirituality in married life. I did so, putting the emphasis on sexual intimacy. But when I finished, Fran begged to respectfully disagree:

> "I just want to say," she began, "that great as marital intimacy with God is, celibate intimacy with Him is even greater. I have been celibate for seven years now, ever since Don's death. And believe me, the intimacy I have with God now is deeper than before. I have experienced something like a resurrection. I have seen the end of the world, survived it, and seen that life does indeed go on afterwards. It not only goes on – it is beautiful."

Fran's experience does not, of course, count against the importance of sexual intimacy. Really, she is confirming that sacrament in an especially striking way. Her husband's death was, for her, "the end of the world." Her world had been her intimacy with Don. And their intimacy had become so deep that she was no longer herself without his physical presence. She had grown into a truly coupled identity through the years of their marriage. She was his wife – that's *who* she was (though she was also a fine mother and successful physician). And so, when Don died, she was no longer herself. The pain of loss when a spouse dies is a measure of the depth to which the spouses have given up their single identities and allowed God to fashion them a coupled identity, to change their hearts.

Couples have even remarked that they don't wish to become too close to each other because it will be too painful when one of them dies. And that is certainly true. Loving anyone makes us vulnerable to that person's death, because love is not just words and actions. Love is a way of being. Love creates ties which are part of the very identities of the people involved. And so, couples who live in true sexual intimacy will find, indeed, that when one of them dies, the other's world will end, too. The one who survives loses his or her very self, loses the identity that was slowly but surely built up in their years together. To lose an identity is just as drastic a change as it was to build it.

But that loss of identity, loss of self, is also a resurrection. As Fran put it so well, she survived. She – Fran, Don's wife – lived on to see that life does, indeed, go on, and that it is beautiful. His death was not so much the loss or destruction of her former self. It was, rather, an expansion of it. Fran found in her widowhood a new intimacy with God. And she found it in her continuing, newly deepened intimacy with her children and with those who had been her friends along with Don. That intimacy was not, however, a celibate intimacy. True, she no longer had Don's physical presence, nor the physical actions by which they exchanged their passionate devotion to each other. But she did have a deeper intimacy with him, and with God, that was marital rather than celibate. For Don had experienced a resurrection, too. For him as for all Christians, dying is not the end of life. It is a passage to a new life. And so, Don lives on, and in some mysterious way is more deeply present to Fran now than he was before his death.

Fran has, of course, lost something very real and important – her husband's physical presence. But he is still present to her, still intimate with her, and she with him. He is no longer bound by time and space as he once was. And so, he is with her wherever she goes, much more freely than he could be before his death. They are no longer separated from time to time as they were in his previous life. They may not converse, may not see or hear each other, or touch each other. But they do have a new and deeper intimacy, one that is just as marital as what they have always had. Sexual intimacy lasts forever.

Fran also gave us some insight into how their intimacy had been built. It had taken many years, years of love and passion, years of work and conversation. But one of the most important times for the growth of their passion was during Don's final illness.

Don spent the final month of his life in the hospital. Against his choice, he was put into a crowded double room. In fact, there was only room for one chair. And so, when Fran would visit him, she often found that the chair was already being used, and there was no place for her to sit. So what did she do?

> "I sat on his bed," she said, "and we would hold hands. Sometimes I would lie beside him, cheek-to-cheek for hours, as we talked. Sometimes we didn't even talk. And I thought about how wonderful that was, and what a blessing that the crowded room forced us into that. If we had been at home, or in a larger room, we probably would not have done all that wonderful touching. Don would have been in his chair, or his bed, and I would have been in my chair. And it wouldn't have occurred to us to lie cheek-to-cheek, or to hold hands for an entire day."

Sexual healing, a sacramental grace, comes about through our sense of touch. Passionate couples touch each other a lot – in fact, they can hardly keep their hands off each other. That desire to touch is a very healthy one. For touching is essential for the growth of any kind of love. Studies have shown that babies who do not get the cuddling and holding, the stroking and hugging they need in the first few months of life, develop fewer brain cells than those who do. That is why doctors recommend that babies be held, and cuddled, when we feed them. Propping a bottle with a blanket so that the baby can nurse alone in its crib may get the milk into the tummy. But babies who are routinely fed that way don't grow and thrive as they should. Their development is stunted, not just emotionally, but physically, too. In fact, when the Frustraci septuplets were born, news reports told us that their oxygen intake increased by 10% when their mother touched them.

Our need for touching is born right into us, and it lasts all our lives. Couples who are in love are following a healthy human instinct when they try to touch each other at every opportunity. They promise to "keep in touch" when they are apart. They are not hesitant about hugging and caressing, because they want to communicate their desire for each other in a constant atmosphere of passion. They seem to be saying, at least to themselves, "I can hardly believe it! Is this real? Or am I imagining things? Do you really love me as I love you? Let me touch you! Let me make sure, once again, that it is real! It seems too good to be true. And yet, it is. Hallelujah!" Our sense of touch is our "touchstone" for what is real and what isn't, especially for the reality of love.

Sometimes the urge to touch each other is a way of giving passion instead of receiving it. We seek to touch something when we are seeking reassurance. But that it a natural impulse when we want to give assurance, too. When a child needs comforting and is standing at some distance from us, we naturally tell him, "Come here, let me hold you." And when a lover needs reassurance – perhaps after a quarrel – we do the same thing. Hugging and holding are powerful body-language. They say, in an especially convincing way, "You are not alone. I am here, close to you. I want to be as close to you as I can. In fact, if I could melt right into you, I would. For you are very precious to me." Passionate couples touch each other, ardently and often, throughout their married life. Hands and arms, lips and laps are parts of the bodies that we give over to each other in our wedding vows. For spouses are human beings, and human beings cannot be in touch unless they touch each other.

We touch each other most intensely, of course, in sexual intercourse. In a later section, we shall see why sexual intercourse is such an appropriate symbol for a sacrament. But more ordinary kinds of touching are healing, too. A simple experiment shows how this is true. Students who checked books out of a college library were surveyed afterwards about their perceptions of the library. They fell into two groups: one group found the library to be a warm and comfortable place, and felt welcome and at home there. The other found it cold and forbidding, an uncomfortable place that they went to only when it was necessary. After the survey, the researchers revealed the difference between the two groups of students. Those who found the library warm and comfortable, who looked forward to going there, had had their hands brushed ever so slightly by the librarians as they checked their books out. Those who found the library cold and forbidding were not touched. They received the same words, the same polite tone of voice, the same prompt and efficient service. But their experience of the library lacked that special human touch. That touch comes only with touching. The first group of students, without knowing why, had been "touched" by their use of the library. The second group had not.

The importance of touch for communicating sexual desire is based on rather ordinary human psychology, then. After all, the main task that all of us face in our Christian life is to come to faith. And faith is, quite simply, believing in the reality of love. All human beings have doubts about that, all our lives long. Some people are outright cynics, going through life believing that love is a fairy tale, an adolescent fantasy. They believe that growing up means becoming "realistic," giving up romantic daydreams. As one of my cynical professors put it, speaking in class one day about love and romance,

> "Here is the ninth beatitude: 'Blessed is he who expects the worst, for he shall not be disappointed!' If he expects the worst, he will either get it, or he won't. If he does, he won't be disappointed, for that is what he expected. If he doesn't get it – if love turns out to be real and not an illusion – he will be pleasantly surprised. In either case, he will not be disappointed."

My cynical professor (who was not, in his real life, as cynical as his "ninth beatitude" would suggest) stated our human fears about the unreality of love in a very clear and forceful way. Those fears lurk in every human heart, and they last all our lives long. Sometimes they are hardly conscious. Sometimes they surface as bitterness, in times of great tragedy, such as the death of a loved one. And sometimes they take a very paradoxical form. For when we have some sort of profoundly healing experience – say, twenty years with a passionate spouse – that makes us believe that love is real after all, that very same comfort and reassurance can bring another kind of fear. Those of us who are blessed with passionate spouses, affectionate children and faithful friends can doubt the reality of love, too. Our doubt takes the form of thinking that it is too good to be true. We don't just think that it *seems* too good to be true. We fear that it *really is* too good to be true, and is, then, not true. We don't trust that reality.

My adopted daughter brought this lesson home to me one day, when she was ten years old. Our family was going out to dinner to celebrate Father's Day, and she suddenly said,

> "Of course, Mother, Daddy isn't our real father."
> A little voice inside me, no doubt that of the Holy Spirit, said, "Be careful with this one, Mom." So I replied, as matter-of-factly as I could, "Yes, he is."
> Mary looked startled, and said, "Huh?"
> I then replied, "Yes, he is. He is a man who loves children, and gives them a happy home to grow up in. And that is a real father."
> "Oh, well. But he didn't bring us into the world. That's real, too, Mother."

"Yes, but I think the other is more real. After all, God is Love, and He is the most real being that there is. So I think that a man who loves children and takes care of them is a more real father than one who brings them into the world and doesn't love them or take care of them."

At that remark, Mary's eyes flashed with anger. She blurted out, "But you don't really know. Maybe my natural father wanted to give me a happy home to grow up in. But he couldn't do it. So he gave me to someone who could. That's love, too, Mother."

What could I say? A little child was leading me. I was learning a lesson about the reality of love from my child. I told her, of course, that she could be right. And I realized that she might well have a double reason to celebrate Father's Day, with two real fathers, both of whom love her.

As I thought about that conversation later on, I saw in my daughter the power, the sacramental, healing power of the sexual passion of her parents. Without our desire for each other, we wouldn't have adopted any children. Little Mary came to us at the age of two months. She was a passive, unsmiling, jumpy baby who startled very easily. We had to pick her up and lay her down gently, and give her lots of cuddling and holding. She had spent her first two months of life with an overworked, busy foster mother who apparently didn't have time to hold her, hug her, cuddle her, and talk to her as much as she needed. And so, we tried to make up for that when she came to live with us. We gave her lots of extra touching. And here she was, ten years later, teaching us something about the reality of love. Our passion had healed her, through the sense of touch.

A deep and solid conviction about the reality of love – the sheer reality of it – is the condition for the heart transplant that Jeremiah recommends. For when we lose our hearts of stone and receive our new hearts of flesh, we experience an utter reversal of our personal identities. We are transformed from self-centered to other-centered in our loving. And that transformation is a real change of personal identities. In this sense, couples come to be sacramental in the same way that anyone else comes to be a Christian. We learn the long, hard lesson of loving someone else instead of just ourselves. We all begin life as little egoists. We think of ourselves, make of ourselves, the centers of our own little worlds. We see and judge everything and everybody in terms of "How does this affect me?" When I try to plan dates and projects for a class, for example, the students almost never think about whether that is good for the class as a whole. Each individual student thinks of his or her desires and interests, his or her convenience, and so on. That is the natural egoism of the human heart. We are born individualists, each of us seeking "Me first," and it is the work of a lifetime to reverse that way of organizing the world around ourselves.

As soon as we fall in love, though, we have a different way of viewing the whole world. When we wake up in the morning, we ask ourselves different questions. It's not, "What shall I do today?" It's "How long until I see Ed? And what will *we* do today?" And if I fantasize different things that we might do, the ones I prefer are not my own inclinations, but Ed's. If someone – one of my friends – says "Let's go to a movie," I don't say "I'd love to." I wonder first if Ed would like to go. If he wouldn't, then I wouldn't, either. And when Ed and I are together, we almost stumble over each other, each trying to please the other. In fact, we easily fall into a hilarious Alphonse and Gaston routine. If we're trying to select a movie, or a restaurant, Ed won't even ask my preference. He knows I won't tell him. Instead, I'll state what I think is his preference. I won't ask him what it is, of course. I'll guess at it, because I know he won't tell me his choice. He'll state what he thinks is mine. Maybe we'll miss a meal, or be too late for the movie, before we make a decision! We're like the two rabbis in the lifeboat, with only one life-saving portion of food between them. Each offers it to the other – "Here, you take it." "No – that would be selfish. You take it." "I can't either – that would be selfish on my part.' And so, they both starve, leaving the food uneaten in the middle of the boat.

These little games are not trivial, though. They are signs that a deep transformation has begun. When we marry, we may find it easy, in our passion to please, to adapt to each other's sexual wishes. Does he want long, slow passion before breakfast, when I feel like going out to jog? Then long, slow passion it will be, for I want what he wants. And gradually, slowly but surely, passion leads to one concession after another. Pretty soon, I find that I don't even think about my preferences. My orientation to life has been reversed. My identity has changed. I no longer think of myself as the single, individual person I used to be. I no longer have "my" day to plan, "my" agenda, "my" life to fit Ed into. My body is not my own.

Psychologists have a name for this mental process, which is at the heart of any person's devotion to another. It is *identification*. It means that in my mind I see another person as my other self. I say to him, "Hello, myself." And I mean it. After a while, I automatically put myself into that other person's place, seeing the world from his point of view, wanting what he wants. And that habit of identification, of decentering my mind and my heart away from myself and toward others, carries over into all my contacts with other people, all day long.

For example, my single self would be upset by a roommate's sloppiness. But my married self isn't. Thanks to passion, I can see that neatness and a sense of responsibility for the house is just not part of my beloved's view of the world. Does he leave his pajamas on the bathroom floor? My single, self-centered, seeking-to-be-loved-rather-than-to-love self would feel hurt and angry. "Don't you care enough about me to do a little thing like hanging up your pajamas?" But my passionate, married, *we*-centered self, seeking not so much to be loved as to love, simply hangs them up – or leaves them on the floor. In either case, it's not a time for "poor me." It's a time to simply see the fact that some people see the world differently from others.

When I am passionately decentered, my mind and heart going out to my spouse, I'm better with my children. On the days when passion has cooled, I need lots of patience with them. They are irritating, and I am irritable. But when passion is aflame, I don't need patience. I have something better – an awesome, almost magical ability to see the world as they do. Did Eddie let the dog out as he went out to play? I don't need to scream, "You know better than that. You did that on purpose! You are grounded for the rest of the day!" No, I realize that a 3-year-old has only one thing on his mind – going out to play with his friends. He isn't even thinking about the dog. And so I can matter-of-factly bring the dog back in, and give Eddie a gentle, affectionate reminder to be more careful about the dog next time he opens the door.

These examples may not seem earth-shaking, but they are the stuff of sexual healing in ordinary married life. When my orientation to the world is decentered, when my *me* identity is turned into a *we* identity, I experience a change in myself that goes with me wherever I go. I take on a new identity, that of a woman whose passion leads her to say – first to her husband and then to everyone else she meets – "Hello, myself." Researchers who have studied child abusers have found that they all have one trait in common. They are not able to identify with children. They cannot, in their imaginations, picture the world from a child's point of view. They see it only from their own viewpoint. And so, they expect children to think as they do, and to behave as they would. When the children do something else instead, the parents feel confused and frustrated. And they act out those feelings in physical violence, in child abuse.

When we consider that children who are abused often grow up to be child abusers themselves, we see how important this one small part of sexual healing can be. Passion is almost a magic potion. It draws our minds away from our narrow view of the world, so that we almost automatically see it the way others do. First we identify with our beloved. But that identification has all kinds of ripple effects, as we see our children, our friends, and even perfect srangers as our other selves.

One day I was walking down the street and heard a woman screaming on the other side of the intersection. Several people were standing nearby watching. I could see a man dragging her toward an apartment building, while she was screaming "No, no! Let me go!" As he neared the door to an apartment, two other men reached out to help him. They began to tear the woman's clothes off. What was I to do? One reaction would be not to get involved. After all, the people were strangers to me. It was none of my business. Probably a domestic quarrel. But something suddenly clicked in my mind. I said to myself, "That woman is in some sort of trouble. And if I were in her place, I would want me to help somehow." And so, I went to the nearest telephone and called the police. They came almost immediately, and went into the apartment. They soon came out. With them was the man who had dragged the woman into the building. His hands were cuffed behind his back. The police put him into their van and took him away. When I asked the officer if he needed me as a witness, he said "No, you can leave." He had seen enough for himself.

What clicked inside me during that episode – the thought that if I were that woman, I would want me to help – was an almost automatic identification. I identified with the woman, saw the situation from her point of view, and decided what to do on the basis of her needs and desires rather than my own. That act of identifying with others, seeing them as our other selves, is the key to the love that is supposed to characterize Christians. We can hardly love our neighbor as ourselves unless we first see our neighbor that way. As I reflected on my actions later on, I could see a bit of growth in myself. That growth, due to my husband's desire for me over the years (and mine for him) was some of the sexual healing that we have been talking about. There was a time in my life when I would not have cared about that woman. I would have passed by, indifferent to her suffering. In fact, there was a time when I would have been one of those standing around watching, satisfying my own selfish curiosity.

The change of identity that spouses, and all other Christians, experience in the life of grace makes such moments of unselfishness into a constant state of mind. Viewing others as our other selves, loving them as we love ourselves, identifying with them and caring about them – these should not just be moments, or striking episodes in our lives. Such love should be our whole way of life. To reach such a constant state of loving is to change so deeply from our inborn selfishness that we can truly say, when it happens, that we acquire new identities. To move from being a self-centered person to being one who is other-centered is, indeed, a conversion – a turning around. Usually we love ourselves first and foremost. We deal with other people in ways that benefit not them, but ourselves. We are often indifferent to others, and sometimes downright hostile. And we are speaking now of ordinary, everyday life. In driving our cars, for example, how often do we even think of other drivers as persons like ourselves, whom we care about as ourselves? Isn't it more likely that we see them as annoying objects that get in our way, cause us trouble and inconvenience? Do we habitually drive so as to make the experience pleasant and convenient for the other drivers? Such a mindset would be the kind of love that would make people sit up and take notice. "See how those Christians love one another!" And it certainly would make defensive driving unnecessary if everyone drove their cars in such a loving fashion.

But what has this to do with sex and marriage, with love and intimacy and sacraments? Plenty! For most people, passion is the force that starts that process of turning them around and keeps it going. In fact, we have to admire the wisdom and ingenuity of our heavenly Father in giving us the gift of passion. Who is more generous and devoted to another than a young man who has just fallen in love? What other force in human life can transform someone more suddenly, shift his focus from himself to another person? What softens a heart more quickly, and more deeply, than falling in love, and staying there? The most strident, angry feminist, once she falls in love, finds that suddenly her rights don't matter. Her concern to be loved, to be treated according to justice, her demands for recognition and equality all melt away. Sexual desire is, indeed, dynamite. Its explosive force blasts open the hard shells of stony hearts, and turns self-primacy into passionate devotion.

Sacramental spouses, then, whose bodies are not their own but each other's, gradually acquire a unity that is truly stunning. They are two in one flesh, one in total belonging, but not just when they make love. That communion is wondrous enough. They are joined in a constant state of interior unity, unity of mind and heart. In a truly astounding mystery, they treat each other as their very own selves all the time. For that is what they are – each other's other selves. They are no longer two persons, living in physical closeness. They are not two individuals pursuing common goals, and sharing common interests. They are not just two people who think alike, who have common principles and share various projects. They are one, not two – so deeply and completely one that they simply cannot think of themselves without each other. They no longer have separate identities.

It is impossible to imagine that people would seek such unity, and achieve it, without sexual desire and passion. It is too hard, too demanding. The very idea of giving up our identity, of putting some other person's needs ahead of our own, is scary and repulsive. To many people, such unity seems in the abstract, cloying and sentimental. To others it is a threat to their autonomy, to their independence and individuality. Why should we give of ourselves to anyone else? How could we ever get enough out of a relationship to justify putting our whole selves into it? What about rugged individualism, and personal self-fulfillment? Who wants to be a martyr? That's stupid. It doesn't get you anywhere.

These questions are precisely the questions of a dispassionate person, one who calculates human relationships in terms of a cost-benefit ratio. And they are precisely the questions that don't even occur in someone who is in love. Just let such a calculator fall in love, and suddenly, the whole picture changes. Rights, independence, fulfillment, an individual identity suddenly fly out the window. The beauty and goodness of the beloved fill the horizon. Kirby in *St. Elmo's Fire* is a perfect example. He was all set to become a lawyer and "make a lot of money," until his eyes met hers. All at once, law school was out, and medical school was in, because medicine seemed the way to win her heart.

Falling in love is more than an episode in a person's life, then. It is a true turning point. Passion is not just a fleeting emotion. It is much deeper and more constant. It brings a change in identity, a new heart. When lovers become passionate spouses, they change their very image of themselves. They no longer see themselves as separate individuals. And the reason why they change their images of themselves is that they change their very selves. They take on new identities. Many people dismiss romance and falling in love as adolescent fantasies. No doubt, that is sometimes the case. Infatuations are common enough. People fall in love with romanticized, false images of each other. They fall in love with love, not with each other. Such people are immature and unrealistic. They create glamorized, perfectionist images of each other. And then, when their illusions are destroyed – as when their beloved makes a mistake, or says something ordinary – their romantic feelings come crashing down to earth. Such people, disappointed in the failure of an infatuation, may even feel cheated. They become suspicious of love itself; they are a little wary, perhaps even withdrawn and bitter.

But the passion that brings about sexual healing is not an immature infatuation. It is just as intense emotionally, but the excitement and desire are realistic. The lovers are drawn to a goodness in each other that is really there. What they desire, whom they desire to belong to, is not a fantasy but a reality. Other people may wonder what they see in each other. But it is there, and they wonder why everyone doesn't see what they see. Other people think they are crazy. But they wonder if everyone else isn't crazy. For they are, in a sense, crazy – crazy about each other. Their very perception of reality is changed, altered. They have been blasted, by the force of passion, out of their ordinary way of seeing the world. They have new mental images of everything. They see themselves differently. They see each other differently. They see the whole world differently. Life has a new meaning.

Those who are cynical about such love, about its reality, like to quote a proverb: "Love is blind." Well, it is. Infatuation is blind, too. But there is a world of difference between these two forms of blindness. Infatuation blocks out certain important realities. A woman who coddles an alcoholic husband, for example, is blind to the fact that her coddling is good for neither of them. She thinks she is loving her spouse, when in reality she is co-operating in his self-destruction. By covering up for him, and taking care of him, and assuming his responsibilities, she makes his cure impossible. Her intentions are good, but her perspective is skewed. She is blind to what her beloved needs from her. She fails to recognize his true good – the inner strength by which he could take responsibility for his cure and bring it about. Since she does not even see – perhaps does not even want to see – that inner goodness, she also fails to support it and affirm it. She doesn't identify with him.

But the blindness of lovers is different. The desire – the headlong, explosive, no-holds-barred desire that is the beginning of sacramental intimacy – is quite different. That blindness is really a selective vision. Passion is a prism. It has a way of focusing our attention on each other's goodness. And the goodness is really there. It is not a figment of anyone's imagination. The faults are there, too. Lovers do not deny each other's faults and imperfections. What they do is to see them in perspective. They are not important. They are not worth any attention. They are not a basis for making choices. Most of all, they are not part of their perception of belonging to each other. In that belonging, they have, instead, a perception of each other's unique goodness – unique in all the world.

My aunt and godmother is a good example. Her husband drank heavily for years. She and her children suffered a great deal from his drinking. And I remember, as a child, overhearing many family conversations in which she was urged to leave him. "The children would be better off with no father at all than with one who neglects them like Fred does," they would say. Or, some would say, "You're a young, attractive woman. You deserve something better. Think of your own happiness." But Aunt Catherine saw something that no one else saw, and that vision drew her to Fred in passion. She saw a special goodness in him. And so, those conversations I overhead always ended with her saying, "No, I want to give him a chance to change." And for ten long years, she gave him that chance.

Catherine was not infatuated. She did not gloss over the horror of Fred's behavior. She did not pretend that he was not an alcoholic. She did not kid herself, or her friends and family, into thinking he was harmless. She saw clearly the damage that he was doing to himself and his loved ones – to her, above all. And she treated his drinking very realistically. She did not make excuses for him, or cover up for him, or assume his responsibilities. She did not grovel before him, slavishly telling him that he was wonderful and that it didn't matter whether he drank or not. She made it very clear that she wanted him to change, and that she was confident that he could. She also made it very clear that she saw the goodness in him.

Fred's goodness was the center of her focus. That is, in her mind, the Fred that she passionately longed for, that she desired to belong to – in fact, that she did already belong to – was not the drunken Fred. It was Fred, the warm, affectionate father. Thanks to her passion for him, and his for her, she was able to see through the alcoholic fog to the real Fred for whom she longed. And after some ten or twelve years, her "blind" love paid off. The healing power of passion won the day, Fred quit drinking, joined AA, and stayed sober for the rest of his life. And in those years of sobriety – about thirty, as I remember – he was a most tender, passionate husband. He was a fine father and grandfather. I knew him and my aunt in their last three years together. They were enjoying an intimacy that was so exquisite that it took my breath away. In fact, I wrote a special note to my mother, thanking her for choosing Aunt Catherine to be my godmother. No one I've known has shown me more clearly the way to faith. And that is just what a godmother is meant to do.

At my last visit with this holy couple, Fred was in the final stages of a fatal lung disease, and had frequent periods when he simply could not get his breath, even with the help of an oxygen tank. After one of those frightening attacks, he said, rather calmly, "Sometimes I think that if I had a gun, I would just shoot myself." Catherine's response was just as calm, and totally matter-of-fact: "Well, if you ever decide to do it, please shoot me first. I really wouldn't care to live without you." She did live, for about a year after Fred died. But she had no heart for living. She lost her appetite, and her tolerance for food. And finally, her heart gave out, weakened by a long struggle with very severe arthritis. But she and Fred showed, as strikingly as anyone I have ever known, the change of identities that passion brings about. Once two people belong to each other in sexual desire, they simply are not the selves, the separate selves, that they once were. And given that kind of intimacy, when one spouse dies, it is not the death of some separate individual for the one who survives. It is a death of the self of the surviving spouse, too.

The blindness of love is not really blindness, then. It is a sharper kind of vision and insight than the "objective" knowledge that is not influenced by feelings. Passion empowers lovers to see each other in perspective, with goodness at the center and everything else at the periphery. Oftentimes, when we deal with the people we are not in love with, we look at them in terms of one part or feature of them. And usually, the feature we look at is one that is useful to us in some way. We look at a bus driver as our means of getting to where we want to go, for example. Or we think of a business partner in terms of the skill or talent he brings to our profit-making enterprise. We rarely take a personal interest in people we don't feel some kind of affection for, even when we treat them fairly and decently. We don't love them as ourselves.

But passion makes everything different. Passion makes us see each other, and see each other whole. We don't look on a passionately desired spouse as a manager or salesman, or as a means of transportation, as a ticket to our education, or an agent of our health and human welfare. We see a passionately desired spouse as some*one*, not as some*thing* – as a person unique in all the world. We may know other people that we like and enjoy, other people that we admire, other people that we find sexually exciting. But with a passionately desired spouse, everything is different. The one we belong to is in a class all by himself, or herself. For the belonging to each other that comes about through passion is not just a matter of feeling, or even of commitment. It is a matter of identity. Who we are to each other is who we are, period. We reach the peak of that identity in those awesome moments of realization when we can only look at our beloved and speak his name, or hers.

Passionate couples often have nicknames for each other, special nicknames that they use only when they are alone. Those nicknames are their way of summing up everything that they mean to each other. Sexual intimacy has a kind of mystic quality about it. But the reverse is true, too. All the great mystics – St. Paul, St. Theresa of Avila, St. John of the Cross – experienced something in the higher states of prayer that they could hardly describe in words. They had some kind of direct, personal contact with God which left them speechless before Him. And later, when they wished to write or speak about that presence, ordinary language broke down. Invariably, they turned to the language of sexual intimacy in their efforts to describe their union with God. The *Song of Solomon* in the Old Testament is a perfect example. Sacramental couples, couples in their sacramental moments, experience something similar. They reach, at times, such a deep insight into each other, such a realization of their presence to each other as the unique persons that they are, that they, too, are at a loss for words. And it is in those mystic moments that a whispered "John!" or "Mary!" or the wordless mouthing of a nickname speaks volumes to the beloved that hears it.

QUESTIONS TO DISCUSS TOGETHER AS A COUPLE

1. Describe a "change of heart" that your passion has brought about.
2. How would you describe the difference between infatuation and sexual intimacy? Give some examples.
3. How can a couple's old age be a time of sexual healing?
4. List some common phrases showing the importance of our sense of touch (like, "Keep in touch," "a touching remark," and so on).
5. Describe a situation in which passion empowered you to identify with another person.

III

The Rise and Fall
of Passion

PROVERBS always contain a kernel of truth. They are not invented out of thin air. Rather, they have their roots in ordinary human experiences. And so, the proverb, "Love is blind," tells us an important truth about all loving human relationships. Whether we love someone or not, and how we act out our love, is determined by how we see that person. If our focus is on faults and failings, we will harp and criticize. We may not associate at all with someone whose faults outweigh their good points. But everybody does have some faults and failings. And so, for love of any kind to happen, there has to be a certain kind of blindness. When love is the kind that we "fall into," when it is the passion or sexual desire that urges two people to belong to each other completely, passion makes them both blind. But that blindness does not deny, or hide, the beloved's faults. It puts them into perspective, a perspective in which the beloved's goodness is central. Lovers even find each other's faults cute or charming. Such is the power of passion to draw people out of their self-primacy into communication.

Faults – some of them not even faults, really, but just differences between people – quickly come to the surface when two people begin to live together. That's when we really find out who's neat and who's sloppy (*The Odd Couple*), who's prompt and who dilly-dallys, who is a morning person and who is a night person. Every couple has to negotiate countless little (and big) practical decisions about where to live, how to spend time and money. They have to make joint decisions. When I went off to get married, my good friend and confessor warned me that most quarrels in married life are about money – how to get it and how to spend it. I soon realized that he was right. But I also saw that those quarrels and disagreements are about money only on the surface. Usually they are about a deeper, hidden issue. After all, disagreements about how to get and spend money are really disagreements about how we spend our time. And the different ways of spending our time are ways of expressing ourselves and being ourselves. Arguments about money, when we get right down to it, involve identity questions. We even use phrases like, "Do you think I'm made of money?" Such competitions, then, are issues of self-primacy. The hidden question in couples' disagreements is always *us*, not *it*.

Take an example. A young couple, newly married, moved to Milwaukee, where the husband was to begin medical school. He knew that his studies would be extremely demanding, and he wished to save as much time as he could for his studies. As he plunged right into his school schedule, he left it to his wife to find them an apartment. "Just one thing," he asked her, "make sure it is within fifteen minutes of the university." As he returned to their hotel after his first day of school, she told him that she had signed a one-year lease for an apartment, and that they would move into it over the weekend. "Wonderful!" he exclaimed. "Where is it?" The address she gave him was at the opposite edge of the city, requiring him to spend several hours each day commuting. The husband, needless to say, was dismayed. "But I asked you to get something within fifteen minutes of the university." "I know," she replied, "but this one has a swimming pool, and I thought that would be nice during hot weather." In his mind, the young husband had to wonder, "Who does she think she is?"

It is easy to see that this disagreement was not about an address, but about time and how to spend it. And conflicts about how to spend time are conflicts about how we are to be ourselves. This young bride had not yet made that marital transition. She was still thinking in terms of "me," not "he," and certainly not "we." In any medical-school marriage, time for the couple to be together to nurture their intimacy is at a premium. It is a great mistake, then, to spend several hours a day travelling instead of being intimate. But this disagreement is quite typical. For all couples, every issue that comes between them is really an issue about their intimacy and how it is to be nurtured. Passion takes people one giant step toward the healing of stubborn "Me" attitudes, towards the belonging to each other that creates a "We."

But that first giant step is just a beginning. We have to continue to follow the lead of passion, along a thousand smaller steps, if we are to reach the goal of sexual healing. The journey toward a sexual intimacy that is prophetic in the church is a long one. It begins with a single step – falling in love. But that step has to lead to thousands of others. And those steps are the seemingly small decisions about apartments, furniture, household chores, recreation, and money.

Decisions about lovemaking are the most important of such "small" steps. When we begin a sexual relationship, many tastes and preferences, many needs and urgencies, many rhythms and responses quickly surface. Here, negotiations are very delicate. For when we put our sexual preferences on the line, we put our very selves on the line in a most vulnerable way. When we fall in love, when we marry, we think we are eager for totally sharing life with each other. But as that total sharing moves out of our fantasy and into reality, it can soon seem pretty frightening. When I tell my spouse, for example, that I like to be touched here but not there, or here but not just yet, I am leaving myself open to several different hurts. He might laugh at my desires, or label them abnormal. He might find them in direct conflict with his own desires and preferences. He might be overly eager to please me, and, in his tense efforts to do so, fail. Or he may simply ignore me. And he makes himself just as vulnerable when he tells me what he likes and doesn't like. We can both be afraid to be so open. And yet, if we aren't, we can't do our best lovemaking. More importantly, we can't build the intimate way of life that can be prophetic in the Church.

There is a very telling scene in *The Breakfast Club*, a movie that portrays a group of teenagers discussing their problems with their parents. One girl's problem was too horrible to even mention, until near the end of the movie. Finally, one of the young men asked her, "What do they do to you?" She whispered, in a tone of horror and grief, "They ignore me." And the young man nodded in perfect understanding. Being ignored by those whose love is important to us can be a devastating experience – not just in our teens, but all our life long. Being ignored precisely as a sexual person, by a passionately desired sexual partner, is one of the worst ways of being ignored. And that is exactly what we make ourselves vulnerable to when we reveal our sexual needs to each other.

The early part of building a life together – the first six months, or a year or two of a marriage – is not the sheer pleasure that we might expect. The pain of making ourselves vulnerable is one we would like to avoid, and, indeed, try to avoid. For most of us, conflict is also painful, particularly conflict with a passionately desired beloved on whom we have bet our one and only life. It is no surprise that couples, usually without realizing it, devise countless little ways to avoid vulnerability and conflict. But of course, there is only one way that we can do that: by avoiding intimacy. And so, we easily fall into patterns of what the mental health professionals call intimacy-avoidance games. We find little ways, in day-to-day life, to keep our desires and preferences concealed, or to impose them on our partner in some kind of psychological bullying. Real negotiation and dialogue, especially in sexual matters, are very rare. And yet, these are the only way to real intimacy.

"Now what does that mean?" Jane was awakened from a sound sleep by Bill's hand under her nightgown, pressing her naked thigh. She didn't say anything yet, or even respond with a gesture. Maybe he wasn't even awake. Maybe he only wanted to touch her as he fell asleep. Maybe he wanted to make love but didn't want her to know that. He had been impotent several times lately, and felt embarrassed. And so, if she didn't know he was trying, she wouldn't know if he failed. Jane wanted to know his intentions, so she could respond. Arouse her own passion? Let him sleep? And yet, in a way, she would just as soon not know. If he didn't know she was awake, he wouldn't expect a passionate response. And so, if none came, neither would have to feel disappointed. Both Jane and Bill need clear signals from each other. Both would like to know what the other has in mind. And yet, both are afraid of such clear signals. If they are open about their desires, they are vulnerable. Typically, Jane and Bill hold back their signals in order to protect their self-esteem. And that, of course, means holding back on their passion.

One important first step in their sexual healing will be a deep unreserved "Yes" to the passion that is drawing them together. And that means some honest and clear communication: "Honey, I'd just like to hold you while I fall asleep." Or, "Let's do it!" The ability to be that open, to trust each other, to face together the possibility that we may try to "do it" and fail, is one of the first healing effects of passion. But in order to experience that trust, we have to make ourselves vulnerable.

Intimacy-avoidance is most common in our sexual relationships.

True, most couples make some basic adjustments in other areas of their shared life. But their sexual patterns are very often a clear model of what the rest of their common life is like. And love-making is important for another reason as well: a couple's sexual relationship is the most important tool they have, the most powerful instrument available to them, for keeping their passion alive. And passion is the source of true marital intimacy. Passion is what heals our self-primacy, our fears of intimacy, our deep desire to "keep ourselves to ourselves." If fears of sexual intimacy are the most deeply felt ones, there is good reason for their being so. For sexual intimacy will, if we let it, lead us down the path toward total vulnerability.

One evening, at supper, my husband put his fork down, looked me in the eye, and said, with some hesitation, "May I say something to you?" I could see that he had something important on his mind, and that he was struggling inside. Part of him wanted to say it, and part of him didn't. We had been married for 9 or 10 years, and I saw the familiar signs: he was afraid to become vulnerable, and yet his desire for me was urging him to do that. And since we were not singles, but pretty well coupled by now, I knew that he was about to ask me for some new vulnerability, too. And so, I would be torn. Part of me wanted to hear his words, and part did not.

I put my fork down, too, and gave Ed my full attention, "Of course, my darling, what is it?"

"I just don't like green beans."

That conversation seems ridiculous, in a way. Anyone who heard it, or who reads about it dispassionately might wonder, "So what's the big deal?" But people who are striving for total sexual intimacy as a way of life, an aura in which they eat their meals, go to work, shop and keep house, will see the point right away. As we avoid intimacy, or postpone it, in order to avoid or postpone being vulnerable, a certain tension builds up. Passion urges us to be more and more open, while self-primacy keeps saying, "Not yet." And so as often as not, for a passionate couple, the fear of intimacy has another side to it. We don't hold back because we are afraid of being hurt. We hold back because we are afraid of hurting each other. We acquire over the years, a delicate sensitivity to each other's sore points.

As our readers can well imagine, in 9 years of our married life, there had been literally dozens of times when Ed had felt like blurting out, "I don't like green beans." But he didn't. Some men don't because they fear being hurt – their wives will laugh at them, ridicule them at the next party, lecture them on the need for a balanced diet, or even forget, and continue serving green beans for the next 30 years. But sometimes the sensitivity goes the other way. Ed was hesitant because he didn't want to hurt my feelings. He only spoke out when he knew that that wouldn't happen. Our years of passion had built a security and trust between us that opened up the "green bean" issue, along with other, more important ones. And I've never served green beans again.

But it's a long, hard road to travel before passion can build our trust and security. We seldom let it have its full sway. Much of our life is a series of "ups and downs" where passion is concerned. Have you ever looked at a couple who have recently fallen in love, noticed their passion, and said to yourself, "Isn't that nice! Too bad it won't last." Did anyone ever say to you, when you were newly in love, "Enjoy it while you can, because soon it will be time to settle down and get serious?" Have you ever seen a couple who were passionately in love with each other, and said, "Just wait until they're married a year." Have you, perhaps, sat in a restaurant, or in a mall, and looked at couples, sorting them out? Did you put the obviously passionate ones into the class of lovers who are not yet married? Have you ever looked at a couple who have been married ten years, or fifteen, been astonished by their desire for each other, and said, "Honestly, you'd think they were newlyweds?" If you can answer "Yes" to any of these questions, you are believing a powerful myth of our culture. And you will have a lot of company.

That myth is that passion isn't meant to last. We *expect* passion to decline when a couple gets married. "We've been living together happily for three years now. Why get married and spoil a great romance?" That statement is often said in a half-joking tone of voice. But for many, if not most of us, it is meant quite seriously. Passion is equated with infatuation. And so, passion is juvenile and immature. We are supposed to grow out of it. When we marry, we are to "settle down" to something better, something more serious and mature. We are to let romance die its natural death, and take on the hard work of dispassionate devotion to duty – cool, calm, and collected.

Of course, couples don't just settle down. They settle *for* what they settle down to. Have you ever taken a nostalgia trip back to the heady days of your first romance? Do you reminisce about the times when you spent all day in each other's arms, went home, and then spent hours on the telephone to each other? Do you feel a twinge of regret for those times when your mind was so absorbed by your beloved that you missed appointments, forgot to eat, lit a second cigarette without realizing that you had done so? Do you put such memories aside with a resigned sigh, saying, "Those days are gone forever. We have more important things to think about now – the house, the children, our jobs. Maybe twenty years from now, when the nest empties, we will have time for each other again?" If so, join the club. You are part of a very common pattern. You have, first, settled down, and then settled for what you settled down to.

But that "settle-down, settle for" pattern is fatal for the sacrament of matrimony. It is a pattern not so much of a smooth, dutiful relationship as of the decline of passion. And passion is the heart and soul of the sacramental symbol. What settling down, and settling for, spouses have lost is not just a certain excitement and joy in living. They have lost the bond that makes them truly a couple. They have lost the healing force which could reverse their self-primacy. They have lost the fire that is going to move them from "Me" thinking to "We" thinking. They have lost the process that nurtures their children and builds the Church. They have lost, to put it bluntly, the prophetic marital quality of their relationship. They are no longer living as spouses, but as congenial roommates. They have what could, in a very real sense, be called a brother–sister relationship instead of a sacramental marriage.

The signs are easy to see. Probably the first to happen is also the most serious: their passion has become episodic. They still find each other sexually exciting, still become aroused for intercourse, still find a satisfactory release in their sexual activity. But their desire for each other only comes alive when they join in sexual intercourse. It is not the atmosphere of their home, the aura in which they live. Passion is more like an oasis in a desert, a moment of refreshment and renewal before returning to the dry dust of daily duties. The many little maneuvers aimed at avoiding vulnerability have worked. Hurts and conflicts have been avoided. But a price has been paid. Passion has faded, and with it, the intimacy that only passion can build.

It is not hard to picture a typical pattern. Few couples actually talk, in any honest and open way, about their sexual desire and the ways to build it. They do what we all do in conversation with someone we have just met: we raise certain topics tentatively, find that we agree on them, and proceed to discuss them at greater length. We raise certain other topics rather tentatively, find that those are areas of disagreement, and then either gloss over the disagreement or avoid the topic altogether. When the "topic" that a couple raise is their sexual feelings, the pattern is even more clear. We avoid certain areas of sexual activity, and sexual conversation, altogether. Sometimes we do that because we don't want to be hurt. Oftentimes we do it because we don't want to hurt each other. And so, desires get suppressed. Suppressed desires lead to a certain degree of anger and resentment. And with the growth of anger and resentment, passion soon begins to fade.

What usually happens, then, is that couples find an acceptable way of making love, and settle into that as a routine. They find a pattern that each can live with, that gives a basic satisfaction. And then they follow that pattern. They don't explore new feelings, or even allow those to develop. They don't try to develop new love-making skills, or even think about what those might be. They find a minimal way for both to be aroused, and then to climax, in a release that is quite mechanical. And that is all there is to it. Their lovemaking, in other words, is minimal. Instead of a gourmet feast, it is a routine meal, a feeding rather than a banquet. And the tip-off is that they relegate their sexual activity to the last place on their list of "things to do today." It is put off until other, "more important" things are done – dishes washed, children bathed and put to bed, dogs walked and plants watered. Then the two come together for lovemaking, even as they set the alarm clock for the beginning of tomorrow's agenda.

Is it any wonder that passion begins to fade? When intercourse becomes just another preoccupation, another item on a busy agenda, passion flares up momentarily, but only to become dormant again until next time. Instead of growing stronger and deeper, the urgency to belong to each other also begins to wane. Self-abandon weakens, and soon we begin to take back, little by little, the selves that we had given over to each other when we ratified our love at our wedding. We become more and more preoccupied with other concerns, and more and more forgetful of each other. Instead of our former eagerness to please each other, we begin to look for what pleases ourselves. We catch ourselves whispering to ourselves, "I know he won't like this, but what the heck – it's only once in a while." Or the whisper may be, "She will understand," or even, "She will just have to understand." We soon find that we can keep our hands off each other as easily as we do our minds.

When we are in the heat of first love, it seems impossible that our minds will someday wander, even in the act of making love. It's not that we imagine fantasy lovers, or affairs. Rather, what we're doing has become so routine that it is boring. And so, we find ourselves planning the next day's menu, the children's dental appointments, or the job calendar for the next month. What has happened to two people whose minds and hearts were once totally full of each other? Of course we thought about menus and appointments then, but there was a difference. Then menus and appointments were in a context of passion. They were the concrete ways of acting out our desire. Passion reached a kind of psychological high point in intercourse, but was just as real, and just as intense, all the rest of our waking moments. It is the passionate aura that has faded.

The side-effects of the decline of passion are not pretty, either. And yet, these, too, are taken for granted by many, many couples. Many assume that "that is the way it is supposed to be." For example, a creeping habit of criticizing each other instead of lavishing praise develops all to easily. We may cringe when we overhear such couples in public – she chiding him for the way he is dressed, he complaining about her failure to call his mother. And yet, we do similar things ourselves. We go to parties and drive home in bored silence. Time was when a party was a time to stay in close touch psychologically, flirting with each other across the room when we happened to be dancing with a friend, or talking with a group. But now, we are more like roommates. We are brother and sister, living together and sharing expenses.

We're not knocking brotherly love, of course. But it is not marital, and hence not the kind of love that couples are called to. And when we speak of these brother/sister marriages, we're not speaking of troubled marriages. The couples we have in mind are devoted to each other. They are kind and considerate, faithful to each other, getting along well, and sharing common interests. One of those common interests, even the chief one, might be raising their children. These spouses enjoy each other's company, and have sexual activity that is frequent enough, and successful enough, to satisfy both. In short, we are not speaking of troubled marriages or those with serious problems. We are speaking of what most people, including the spouses, would call "good" marriages – stable, peaceful, fruitful and affectionate. But they lack that special spark, rather, steady flame of passion. And passion is the distinctive mark of a sacramental marriage. Without it, there can be a lot of love in a household, but the love is not marital. It is fraternal, sisterly. And it is not prophetic in the church.

Picture a typical marriage in which one spouse works outside the home – or, to be contemporary, both do. The Huxtables on The Cosby Show will do. In a recent episode, Clare came home from her law office flushed with a joy at a triumph she had scored in court that day. One by one, family members, including her husband, declined to let her tell them about it. They were all preoccupied with something else. (Cliff, her husband, was pre-occupied with the death of their youngest daughter's pet goldfish. He was intent on comforting the girl, and staging an elaborate family funeral for her fish.) But by the end of the evening, Cliff had realized his mistake. He stopped ignoring his bride, and took deliberate steps to give her his full affectionate, teasing attention. He finally did what nearly all couples need to do – renew their intimacy after being separated by the day's work.

Passion fades, often enough, because of our neglect about things which may not seem very important. Entrances and exits are such occasions – the many times when we leave each other's company to go to work, to school, to the store, and so on, and then return home to be together again. When a couple are in love, they are so constantly alert to each other's whereabouts that they say "Hello" and "Good-bye" ardently at every separation and reunion. But when passion fades, a wife may not even know whether her husband has left yet for work. A dispassionate husband may answer the telephone, learn that the call is for his wife, and not know whether she is in the house or not without asking the children. Leaving each other's company without saying "Good-bye" is one of the bad habits that mark creeping dispassion. Returning to each other's company without notice, or with a perfunctory, preoccupied kiss is another.

As time goes on, the situation gets worse. Self-perceptions begin to change. Joe no longer thinks of himself as Maria's beloved, but as a salesman, mechanic, lawyer, perhaps as father to his children. He identifies himself in terms of his work. Maria's self-perception changes, too. She no longer identifies herself as Joe's beloved. She gradually forgets – not the fact that she is married to him, of course, but the realization, the constant desire for Joe that once marked every moment of her life. What was once in the forefront of both their minds gradually fades into the back-ground. And so, their daily separations have a cumulative effect.

As self-perceptions change, so do identities. Joe's work is no longer his way of supporting his intimacy with Mary. It is his life. He brings his work home with him, even when he doesn't need to. If he doesn't do that literally, he at least brings it home in his mind. It is all he thinks about. And so, his association with Mary, their home life, eventually becomes the support-system for his job, rather than the other way around.

And where is Mary in all of this? Let's remember that people are present not where they are physically, but where their minds and hearts are. The proverb, "Home is Where the Heart Is" can be read in two different ways. For passionate couples, their home is the seat of their passion. Wherever they go, however poor the surroundings, since they carry each other in their hearts, they are "at home" with each other. They are intimate, united in passionate devotion, even when they are physically far apart. They carry their home to work with them or to school, or wherever they may go, because they carry each other. But with a dispassionate couple, fraternal love creates a distance. Their hearts are somewhere else – his at work, hers, perhaps, with the children. And so, even when they are very close to each other physically, in the same house, the same room, even the same bed, they are far apart in mind and heart. They aren't "at home" with each other, because home isn't where their hearts are. Haven't we all said "Sorry, I was a thousand miles away?" Of course we are only inches away when we say that, as far as our bodily presence is concerned. But our mind has wandered, and perhaps our hearts as well. And so, our personal presence was lacking. When couples allow their passion to decline, they don't just find their minds wandering during an occasional conversation. They find them wandering, incredible as it may seem, even when they're making love. They forget who they are. Their marital identity becomes as dormant as their passion, revived for brief episodes of sexual arousal.

Haven't we heard the proverb – perhaps even used it ourselves – "O.K., I took him for better or worse, but not for lunch every day." The proverb refers to men who have retired from their jobs and are now at home all day, every day. Their wives complain that they get underfoot. Many men get sick, and even die, shortly after they retire. Others retire psychologically, becoming depressed and withdrawn. Oftentimes, these problems all stem from one basic mistake: that the men and their wives retired from passion early in their married life. They may have done so with the best of intentions. They may have simply assumed, without even thinking about it, that that was expected of them. But it was a mistake nonetheless, and one which has long range consequences. And as likely as not, both spouses collaborate in the decline of their passion. When a man identifies with his work rather than with his wife, she can find a quite pleasant independence, a freedom to be her separate self with all the security of his financial support.

One of my friends said it very clearly one day – almost too clearly. She is an intelligent and educated woman, working as a high school teacher and raising seven children. Her husband is a busy lawyer. To an observer, they certainly have a good, stable, happy marriage. But they are living out the expectations of the culture. As Jenny told me one day, sex and passion are totally unimportant for their relationship!

> We are simply two persons who like each other very much. We are very good friends. The fact that we are able to have children is a nice bonus, but it is really beside the point as far as our relationship is concerned."

I've wished that I could have pursued that conversation a little further, for Jenny and Frank impress me as a couple with plenty of passion between them. But Jenny was hurt, by some of the negative attitudes toward sex that we hear all too often in the Church. She is also a feminist, although one of those few feminists who crusade against abortion. And she is right in seeing the value of her marriage to Frank not in terms of their having children, but as a relationship between her and her husband. There is a little confusion, though, in saying that sex is irrelevant to a marriage. Sex certainly is not for the sake of reproduction in the simple biological sense of that term. Nor should sexual differences be the basis for unequal treatment which denies the equality of men and women. But after all that is said, sex is still important. It is essential to a sacramental marriage. It is the difference which makes a difference.

Would it be too extreme to say that those couples whose passion has cooled are living together without being married? We think not. Such couples have been through a ceremony. They are ritually married. But they don't have the new, coupled identity that the marriage vows call for. They may assume that new identity for a while. But they soon fall back into their separate, pre-marital ways of thinking of themselves, and of being themselves. Except for more or less frequent episodes, they are, in the words of Barbara Mandrell's song, "sleeping single in a double bed." They have the psychological equivalent of an on-again, off-again marriage. Not that they fight and then make up, or separate and then unite again. But they only assume that inward attitude of a couple – passion, that is – for a few brief moments now and then, and then lay it aside as they become preoccupied with other things.

But matrimony is a sexual sacrament. It is a sexual way of life. It is not a friendship with sex, nor fraternal charity with sex. Nor is it respect, affection, and generosity with sex. It is, rather, sexual generosity, passionate kindness, urgent, ardent respect. So central are passion and desire to a sacramental marriage that we can truly say that the decline of passion is a kind of infidelity. True, the couples whose passion fades do not have sexual intercourse with anyone except each other. So, they are not adulterers in that sense. But they are unfaithful to each other in a deeper and more important way. After all, what did their marriage vows say? What were those words so full of passion that we wondered whether we would say them correctly, and even wondered afterwards whether we had? Did we solemnly, and excitedly, promise, "I will never sleep with anyone else?" Were we thrilled to hear our partner say, "I have certain principles, and my own integrity as a person, and I will never violate these"? Hardly. Those formulas don't give us the feeling that someone is crazy about us, that we are irresistible. Integrity and principles make pretty cold bed partners. A heart that doesn't belong to another woman, or to another man, might belong instead to golf buddies and bridge partners.

Fidelity really means constancy, constancy of passion, constancy of desire. It means living, all day and every day, what the vows say: "to have and to hold." That phrase has powerful sexual connotations. It refers to the total abandonment of ourselves to each other, that reaches a kind of high point in intercourse but also marks every waking moment – and the sleeping ones, too. It means having each other, and holding each other – which is a permanent state of having each other – in the obvious physical sense of those terms. And in no other action do we have and hold each other as passionately as in our sexual embraces. But those embraces include an inner, psychological way of having and holding each other that is the constant of our life together. And that is the passionate fantasizing, the desire for each other, that is the aura of every thought and action, every decision and intention, whether we are in each other's arms or not. When a man and woman are in love, they cannot think of each other without being excited. And it is that constant excitement, along with our physical coupling, that we promised when we promised "to have and to hold."

I have wondered for years, both for my life and for the students I teach, why sexual intercourse is such an important action. There is no doubt that it is important. One of the most important things we want to know, about all the people we know and all the new people we meet, is their sexual status. One of our constant topics of conversation about people is who is sexually available and who is not – who is married to whom, who is single but looking, who is vowed to celibacy. Another of our fascinations with people is whether they are sexually initiated or not, whether they have had that important first experience of sexual intercourse. That first, our "loss" of our virginity, is more important than any other "first" in our lives. We all experience our first time to roll over, to sit up without support, to hold our own bottles, to walk, to talk. We go through our first day of school, our first job, our first time to drive a car. But none of those "firsts" has the impact of our first sexual experience. (Sometimes our first sexual experience doesn't have as much impact as later ones, but that is another story). At any rate, a person's sexual initiation is the topic of high art. It is the theme of serious novels, poems, movies, and operas. Why? What is it about that action which makes it so different from other human experiences, even very powerful ones like birth and death?

The best answer I've been able to formulate so far is that sexual intercourse is a naturally symbolic action that touches the deepest dream of the human heart. That is why it is so powerful: it either confirms that dream, more convincingly than anything else we can do to confirm it. Or else it contradicts the dream, also in a very convincing way. And the reason why intercourse has that power is the way in which it involves our entire selves – body and mind, senses, emotions, will. And basic to that involvement is our very intense use of the sense of touch in the act of making love.

The dream I refer to, the deepest dream of every human heart, is a desire so deep, and so strong, that we almost hesitate to speak it, even to ourselves. We are afraid that it cannot come true. We are afraid that it is too good to be true. The dream, shared by men and women alike, is that we might be loved, totally and unconditionally, with no strings attached, just for being who we are. And the love must come from someone who knows us exactly as we are. It can't have any false basis. It cannot be an acceptance of the self I pretend to be, but of the self that I am. And the one who knows me as I am, and affirms me just for being who I am, must be able, and willing, to affirm my true self for my sake. I do not want to be used, to be treasured by someone because I meet one or more of that someone's needs. The love has to be given for my sake, and with total freedom. Does that sound like the Prince Charming story? In a way, it is. I want a love that comes as a free gift, without my asking for it or doing anything to deserve it. And I want it to come from someone whose motives are pure, whose own goodness is so great that he or she doesn't need to use me.

The question, of course, is whether that is an empty dream, or one that I might realistically hope to have fulfilled. Is the fairy tale one that I must grow out of? Is the dream one of the childish things I should put aside, along with my dolls and tricycle, when I assume the serious responsibilities of adult life? Must I, in order to be realistic, become somewhat cynical about the reality of human love? Not a complete cynic, of course, because it certainly seems that some people do love some people, some of the time. And sometimes the love is given freely, without any admixture of self-interested motives. But isn't it foolish and naive to believe that someone can love someone else in constant fidelity, in a state or condition of ecstatic delight in the that beloved's goodness, affirming and supporting it purely for its own sake? Or is it?

The power of the act of sexual intercourse lies right here: for it is one of two things. It is either a most convincing support for the dream, a promise that it will come true, a statement that, indeed, it has already come true. Or else it is an equally convincing betrayal of that dream. In that action of intercourse we find the clearest test of something that is the Number 1 concern of every human being throughout his or her life: the reality of human love. Without that special symbolic content, the action is just like the couplings of all other mammals. An erect penis enters the vagina and deposits therein the male reproductive cells. Looked at from this purely physical point of view, sexual intercourse is just one of many wonderful things that organisms do. But it is no more wondrous than, say, nourishment and growth, the metabolism of food and excretion of wastes.

But consider the psychology of the sexual coupling of human beings, who look at each other from the perspective of a common dream, the reality of love. We look for evidence of that reality in all of our interactions with each other. Without even thinking about it, we make decisions, in every encounter with every person we meet, about whether that person is helping or hurting us, loving us or using us. When we do find ourselves giving and receiving genuine love, what do we find? As one who sometimes gives love, I find myself decentered in my personal powers, my mind and will. I decenter my attention, turning it away from myself and toward the person I love. After all, I can't love someone I don't know, or someone I don't think about. In fact, the more I love someone, the more fascinated and preoccupied I am with that person, and the more forgetful I am of myself. My will, too, is decentered, my ability to decide for myself how I shall act. When I love someone, I act in one way rather than another because of the one I love. I don't center my willing on myself. What I do and say is, instead, centered on my beloved. I seek what is good for him or her. In fact, the more I love someone, the more my concern is centered on the one I love, and the less I care for myself.

In any act of love, then – like giving information to a stranger on the street, or sending a Mother's Day card – the two key features of genuine love are the two elements of self-abandon. Any kind of loving consists in turning my mind and heart, myself, over to the one I love. Whenever we find these features lacking – when someone claims to love us, but thinks about and cares for himself instead, we are immediately suspicious that we are being used rather than loved. Real love is marked by self-abandon on the part of the lover. Otherwise it is not real love.

The power of the act of sexual intercourse comes, then, from its ecstatic character. For at the moment of sexual release, at the climax of sexual intercourse known as orgasm, we reach a psychological peak of self-abandon. In all other acts of loving, I do, to a certain extent, decenter my attention and my concern, turning these away from myself and toward the one I love. But in these other, more ordinary actions, my self-abandon is not complete. My attention may be almost totally on the person I love, but some little bit of it remains fixed on myself. I know, at least in the fringes of my mind, who I am and what I am doing. I keep some measure of self-awareness. Likewise, my will, my concern, my decision-making power is turned away from myself and toward the one I love. I don't do and say what suits my needs, but give myself over to the needs of the one I love. But again, in these other, more ordinary acts of love, my self-abandon is not complete. While my concern may be almost totally focused on the one I love, I do keep some measure of self-control, some ability to change my words and actions so that they suit my needs and desires rather than those of the one I love. What begins as an act of love can change very quickly into one of using.

But in sexual intercourse, these last shreds of self-awareness and self-control disappear. At the moment of sexual release, it is psychologically impossible to withhold either mind or will. We do lose that last little bit of self-awareness, forgetting, for the moment, who and where we are and what we are doing. (The French call orgasm *"le petit mort,"* the little death). We also lose that last little shred of self-control, as we do and say things we would never dream of doing or saying in our ordinary frame of mind. We do not, cannot control ourselves, and do not wish to. Psychologically, then, self-abandon, the giving of self over to a loved one, is as complete as it can ever be in the ecstasy of intercourse. That action, when it is performed by human beings rather than other animals, says something more than the transfer of sperm from one body to another. It says love, self-abandon, the complete gift of oneself to another.

And that is why sexual intercourse is such a powerful experience in human life. It either means what it says, or it doesn't. When two people who mean what they say engage in sexual activity, they end up saying what they mean, in the most powerful way that we know – the ecstatic abandon of their very selves to each other, in love. For such couples, the dream of their hearts is fulfilled. For one brief but intense moment, they are loved, and know that they are loved, freely, generously, and for their own sakes. And they love each other, they give love, in the same way that they receive it – in total self-abandon. There is simply no other human experience in which people feel themselves, with such intensity, giving and receiving what all of us dream of giving and receiving – love with no strings, simply because someone who knows us as we are finds our goodness irresistible. And the negative power of intercourse has its roots here, too. When we engage in sexual activity without love, whether we are the user, the used, or both, we have a most vivid denial of love. Using someone as a sex object is the most profound, and the most convincing denial of that peson's goodness that can be found anywhere in human experience.

And how, then, does passion as a way of life become so powerful? Why is the aura of sexual desire a force for healing, for unifying, for converting us away from "Me" and moving us toward "We?" Because the aura of passion simply continues the promise made in intercourse. Passionate couples, keeping their sexual desire alive, live in a constant state of abandoning themselves to each other. And in that self-abandoning love, they confirm, again and again, each other's fondest dream. They show each other, in one gesture after another, "I find you irresistible. You are so good, that I want you to exist, and be yourself, just for your own sake. And don't you forget, I know that goodness better than anyone else in the whole world. For I know you better than any one else in the whole world." And couples who allow their passion to decline lose something precious beyond words. For their intercourse does not mean what it says. The self-abandon which they experience momentarily in the act of making love doesn't carry over into the rest of their life. It stays in the bedroom. What their intercourse says, then, goes against the natural symbolism of that action. For they do not mean to say "I love you with total abandon." Instead they say, "I, who know you better than anyone else, do not find your goodness totally irresistible. I want it for myself, but only at certain times, and only under certain conditions. I see your goodness as good for me. And that is why I want to be with you." When we allow our passion to decline, we are not decentered. We reinforce our fixations on "Me," instead of turning toward "We." We deny and weaken the dream of our hearts.

Isn't it obvious, then, that we make a big mistake when we let our passion cool? When our desire for each other becomes episodic, we keep making a promise and then taking it back. In the bedroom, we say, "I'm all yours and you're all mine." We confirm each other's dream. But then, when we leave the bedroom, it's as if we say, "Well, I didn't really mean that. I was carried away." And so we weaken the dream. Pretty soon, we decide it is not so real, after all. We don't believe the self-abandon of intercourse. We settle into a polite, kind, stable, dutiful relationship that has lost its spark and excitement.

What's really lost, though, is the sexual healing that comes about when we keep the flames of passion burning. For when we live in an aura of sexual desire, every gesture, every word, every look confirms the dream. And we ourselves become prophetic. Who we are – the marital identity we take on – confirms the dream for everyone, in the Church and beyond.

The question, then for all of us – the ongoing question for anyone who thinks at all about the meaning of human life – is, "Is love real, or isn't it?" Sexual passion, lived as an aura whose culmination is in intercourse, is the most powerful affirmation that we have of the reality of love. And that power is due to our sense of touch. After all, if we were pure spirits, like angels, some other experience would be more powerful. We would find love affirmed in our purely intellectual, purely spiritual activities. But we are part of the animal kingdom. We are sexed, and sexual, beings. And so, we are not just minds and wills. We have our senses and our emotions to put us into contact with the world in which we live, the world of bodies, human and otherwise. In many areas of our life, our senses sometimes deceive us. They make us think that something is real when it really isn't. That pavement up ahead looks wet. Is it really? One touch is all it takes to tell us that we saw an optical illusion. The music box seems to be playing. Is it really? One touch tells us that it is, as we feel the vibrations. Time and again, we use our sense of touch to correct our other senses. Eyes and ears, nose and tongue might deceive us from time to time, but touch will set us right. Touch is our most direct and immediate contact with the physical world.

It is also our most direct and immediate contact with that all-important dream, that all-important reality, human love. That person seems to love us, and to accept the love that we give. The face that we see, the words that we hear, would seem to indicate that. But is that love real or only illusory? Once again, touch comes to the rescue. And the most "touching" experience of all, the linking of two whole bodies in the ecstasy of sexual intercourse, is the most powerful sign. When we mean what we say in intercourse, we say the same thing – and mean it – outside the bedroom. And it is that ongoing passion that counts. When we keep our passion alive, we confirm the dream all day long. My choice of vegetables for supper – spinach instead of green beans – says as much as my lovemaking does. It says, "Yes, go ahead and believe it. You are loved, just for being who you are, by someone who sees your goodness more clearly than you see it yourself."

One day when I was rather deeply discouraged, I met a friend by accident on our campus. He is a very perceptive man, one we've known and loved for twenty years. He asked about Ed. When I said, "He's just fine," our friend said, out of the blue, "You know, I understand what it is that you see in him." With that remark, my discouragement lifted at once. And my passion was instantly renewed. It was like hearing my prophecy come back to me. For when lovers dare to let their passion carry the day, all of life is different. As we see the reality of human love in each other, we see it in other people too. We see it wherever it is. And then we can declare what we see.

Isn't that what prophecy is all about? Prophets have a message, a message that their very selves proclaim. And for passionate couples as for Jeremiah, Hosea, and Jesus, the message is always the same:

> God is Love,
> And he who
> Abides in love
> Abides in God,
> And God in Him. (I John, 4:16)

QUESTIONS TO DISCUSS TOGETHER AS A COUPLE

1. Why should Catholic couples strive to improve their lovemaking skills? How might they go about it?
2. Name some signs that passion is beginning to cool.
3. Name some ways that couples might use to carry their sexual intimacy beyond the bedroom, into their entire home.
4. Give several examples of how spouses could make their "entrances" and "exits" more passionate.

IV

Isn't it
A Shame?

I recently asked couples in a parents' class at my son's Jesuit high school to give themselves the following little quiz:
1. Name the most spiritual couple you know.
2. Name the most romantic couple you know.
3. Name the most passionate couple you know.
4. Name the most Catholic couple you know.

Then, without having any names named, I asked them for adjectives that they would use to describe those various couples. To no one's surprise, the most spiritual couples were seen as prayerful, as frequent Church-goers, as active in parish organizations, as making annual retreats and regularly reading religious books and magazines. The romantic couples were very emotional, excited about each other, aware of each other, somewhat dreamy-eyed and immature. The passionate couples were just what the term suggests – sexually attracted to, and excited by, each other, given to flirtatious looks and gestures, highly aware of each other all the time, eager to be in each other's company and physically "in touch" with each other. And the most Catholic couples were – you guessed it! – conservative, moralistic, schooled in rigid rules about sexual behavior and faithful to those rules – but neither passionate nor romantic. Instead, they were dutiful, rational, restrained in all emotion, including sexual excitement. They tended to be self-righteous and judgmental toward others who did not share their view. They made moralistic duty the focus of their lives.

Most Catholic couples would respond to the quiz in much the

same ways. And most would respond in the same way to my next question: 5. How many of you named the very same couple for all four questions? How many of you named one, and only one, couple as being outstanding for both passion and spirituality, both romance and Catholicity, for having all four sets of qualities in an outstanding, attention-getting degree? Of course, none of my couples had answered the questions that way. Very few, in a typical group of Catholic couples, would. We usually put morality and romance into separate compartments. We might combine spirituality and morality in the same couples, or passion and romance. But all four? Passion *and* spirituality? Romance *and* morality? Passion *and* romance *and* spirituality *and* morality? Never. How could anybody combine such contradictory features? To be spiritual is to be above anything that has to do with the body, especially sex and passion. To be passionate, sexy and romantic is to lean strongly in the direction of immorality, to be unspiritual. Sex and prayer just don't go together. Sex and holiness cannot be combined.

That compartmentalizing is precisely the problem we wish to address. And we want to address it in the strongest possible terms. We insist that for a sacramental couple, sexual passion and spirituality do not just go together. They have to be combined. There is no marital holiness that is not passionate. In fact, the law of marital holiness is, "the holier we are as a couple, the more passionate we should be. The more we want to be morally good, the more we must cultivate our romance." The way – the only way for a sacramental couple to be spiritual is to be passionate and romantic. The only correct morality for Catholic married couples is the morality which leads them to make the most of passion and romance, not to put the brakes on. And when passion and romance are at their height, so are spirituality and moral goodness.

Isn't that what the symbolism of sexual intercourse means? Our spiritual life is our life in the Spirit, the life in which we love God with our whole hearts, our whole minds, and our whole strength. It is the life in which we love our neighbor as ourselves. But for holy couples, the high point of love for God and neighbor is the moment of sexual ecstasy. And that ecstasy, carried over into daily life, is the passionate aura of holiness. It is the context of their constant state of loving. What we are to each other in making love is what we wish to be to each other all the time. And what we are to each other is what we are to the church and the world.

But what about prayer? What about religious practices? What about moral goodness? The conclusion is simple. For sacramental couples, *sexual intimacy is prayer.* Sexual intimacy is our most important religious practice. Books and magazines about sexual intimacy are essential parts of our spiritual reading. Falling into love was our grace of vocation, the beginning of our sacramental life. And so, our continuing love, our growing sexual desire and passion for each other, is the growth of that sacramental life. It's not just that being married makes sexual desire and sexual ecstasy legitimate for couples. A wedding doesn't just give us permission to enjoy sex. And it is not just that, being married, we can pray, make retreats, go to Church, give money to the poor and so on, even though we also have sexual intercourse from time to time. No, the connection is much closer than that. When couples pray, make retreats, go to Church, help the poor, and so on – whenever we do whatever we do – sexual passion provides our aura of holiness.

And so, it has to follow: The most passionate couple we know *is* the most spiritual couple, and *vice versa.* And the most romantic couple we know is the best morally. All of these are one and the same couple. And just as passion is the aura in which we pray, passion should also be the main thing we pray for. Maybe we don't think we need to do that. Maybe we think we are passionate enough, and always will be. But God's grace (and passion is a grace) is never securely ours. It can weaken and die. It can also grow, no matter how intense it may be now. And so, we do need to pray for it, every single day.

What's that? You don't want to pray for passion? You like being cool and in control? Most of us do. In fact, wives have a proverb that we use in our conversation with each other: "I've got him wrapped around my little finger." That proverb means, "I'm in control. I know how to get anything I want out of him. And I intend to stay that way."

There's only one way for a wife to stay in control of her husband, however. She has to keep her passion cool and his hot. If she ever lets herself get carried away, control will be the furthest thing from her mind. Her passion will lead her to melt in his arms. On the other hand, if his passion for her ever cools, her control will be impossible. He will be a stone wall in resisting her wishes. To use the common, somewhat vulgar phrase that knowing women use, "when he's hard, he's soft. But when he's soft, boy, is he ever hard."

But who wants control? That's just the opposite of intimacy. The fact that we have to kill passion in order to exercise control is a clear enough sign. Passion means ecstasy, a state of totally vulnerable self-abandon. That's at the heart of the prophetic intimacy of a sacramental marriage. And so, let's pray for passion. If we think we don't need it, let's let God surprise us. Ask Him for more. If we find we don't want it, then we need it more than ever. Let's pray to want it. And then pray to feel it, and to live it.

The liturgy encourages us to do that, if we pray with marital hearts. Just to take an example at random, what couple could say the following prayer without making it a prayer for passion?

> God our Father, open our eyes to see your hand at work in the splendor of creation, in the beauty of human life. Touched by your hand, our world is holy. Help us to cherish the gifts that surround us, to share your blessings with our brothers and sisters, and to experience the joy of life in your presence. We ask this through Christ our Lord. Amen

(Prayer for Seventeenth Sunday in Ordinary Time).

What makes a spiritual couple outstanding for their spirituality, then, should not be how often they pray, but how deeply they love – and the depth of love is made of passion. Further, what makes a couple morally good is not the dutiful keeping of rules and regulations, but their passion, which enables them to love God and neighbor. We can apply the slogan of a cigarette ad right here: "Don't let anything, ever, be ordinary." For a sacramental couple, every moment of every day is extraordinary. Every word, every gesture, every decision is special because the two belong to each other in passion. When something does become ordinary – and we mean anything at all, even washing dishes and paying bills – it is only because passion has faded.

When that happens, it's a very safe bet that lovemaking has also become ordinary. When sex becomes routine and dull, the couple have fallen for the myth of our culture, a myth that is profoundly anti-Christian. That myth is that love is an illusion, an adolescent fantasy, and that married life is supposed to kill passion. But we know that passion does decline, for most couples. How can that be? Why does it happen? Part of the reason is the influence of our culture. It is not easy for sacramental couples to be "in the world but not of it." But there is a deeper question, too. What is it in human beings that makes the myth of the decline of passion so well-accepted? What is it in us that allows us to find that myth so believable? It almost seems at times that we want to disbelieve in the reality of love. Life seems easier, less demanding that way. If we don't have a dream, we won't be disappointed. And we won't have to work so hard, either.

The Bible, in its very first book, gives us an answer. Our disbelief in the reality of love, our willingness to let our passion cool, is a result of the sin of Adam and Eve. We allow sexual passion to fade and even die because we don't really believe in the reality of love. And that disbelief is the most common way for married couples to share in the sin of the first couple. The story of Adam and Eve puts that sinful tendency into a single word: shame. Before their disobedience, Adam and Eve were naked and not ashamed. After their disobedience, they made fig leaves to hide themselves – their sexual organs – from each other. And they hid themselves from God, too. Instead of the open self-abandon that had marked their early life with each other, they began to hide and withhold themselves. And that is exactly what we do when we let our passion cool. We become less totally abandoned to each other. We hold something back, keep something hidden from each other. We keep some of our selves for ourselves. We also hide from God, as did Adam and Eve. Instead of the totally ecstatic love of God that marks passionate couples, we show a certain dutiful restraint. Fear creeps in when passion begins to fade.

Biblical scholars tell us, of course, that the story of Adam and Eve is not meant to be history. It is not an actual event that happened to two real individuals who were the first man and the first woman. Rather, the story is symbolic. Adam and Eve represent all of us. Their story is not factual. But it is meant to symbolize something that is factual: the shame that plagues every human being who tries to give love, who tries to accept love, who tries to believe in the reality of love. The symbolic story has two stages, one before the sin of disobedience and one after. This symbolic "before and after" story is meant to tell us that our present (after) way of doing things is different from the ideal (before) way in which we ought to do them. Now, we live in shame – a shame that takes the form, in our marriage, of letting passion fade. The way we ought to live is without shame – naked before each other, naked together before the God who created us to live together in love. For sacramental couples, that ideal way of living, of being naked and not ashamed, is the life of constantly growing desire. It is the aura of passion.

For sacramental couples, sexual ecstasy is a supreme moment of being together. In that moment, we fulfill God's purpose in making the second human being, Eve. God made a second human being, one who was the sexual opposite of the first one, because "it is not good for man to be alone." And so, the moment of sexual ecstasy is a symbol, a sacramental symbol. As a sacramental symbol, it causes what it symbolizes. And what is that? The ongoing ecstasy, the constancy of passion, that permeates the lovers' whole life together like a mist. Those who are naked and not ashamed live in constant desire and self-abandon. Adam's cry of welcome to Eve when he first met her says it perfectly: "Bone of my bone and flesh of my flesh!" Could there by any language that could say more clearly, "Here is my other self, cherished and loved as I love myself?" "Bone of my bone and flesh of my flesh" is the motto of every sacramental couple. And physical nakedness is the symbol of the much more important psychological nakedness that passion leads us into.

That shame that Adam and Eve felt after their disobedience, the same shame that leads all of us to avoid intimacy, is not the embarrassment of having someone see our naked bodies. That is one kind of shame, and it probably does play some role for some couples in restraining their passion. But the shame and nakedness that are really important are much deeper. Shame in its more serious sense is the deep sense of our unworthiness as persons. It is a psychological shame, a fear of revealing our thoughts and feelings to another person. We are ashamed of ourselves and afraid that we might be hurt if we let someone else see those deeper selves as they really are. That hurt can take many forms. We might be laughed at, rejected, or simply ignored. And so, to protect ourselves against those hurts, we keep ourselves to ourselves. People can't laugh at something that they don't even know about. They can't reject what they're not aware of, can't be accused of ignoring something that they didn't even know about.

Take a simple example – simple, but significant. Most couples find some difficulty in talking honesty and openly about their sexual feelings. Do I dislike lovemaking in the early morning, when I am still groggy and half asleep? That is an important fact for my spouse to know. But he can't know until I tell him. And I might not wish to tell him. I might be afraid that he will taunt me. (One husband I know said to his wife, "Your problem is that you're not a night person, and you're not a morning person either. You're not any kind of person at all." That hurt.) Or I might be afraid that my husband prefers early morning sex to any other kind, and so we will have a conflict to work out. I may be afraid that he will take my dislike of early morning sex as a personal rejection. Or I might tell him of my feelings and find that he simply ignores them. There are many possible unpleasant, and even painful consequences that might come from that apparently simple revelation of my preferences about the time of making love. And so, to avoid those consequences, I might simply keep those feelings to myself. But if I don't tell my spouse, he will never know. And then, he will not have the opportunity for making love in the way that delights me the most.

The result of my withholding that little piece of information is not little at all. It is a significant cooling of our passion, and thus a defect in our intimacy, at the very least. More likely, some worse consequences will eventually follow. My husband will be disappointed that my self-abandon in the morning is not as wild as he would like. He may begin to doubt my love for him, and his own lovability. And I will begin to feel, and to store up, resentment that sex is always when he wants it, and never when I do. My resentment and his self-doubt could soon become very serious enemies of our passion. We will not share our breakfast in passionate, relaxed ecstasy but in a tense politeness. We will part for the day with some small sense of relief rather than regret. We will be glad to get into the day's agenda so as to get our minds off each other – the very opposite of living in an aura of passion.

This example is one of many that would show how couples must deliberately cultivate passion through honestly revealing their sexual feelings to each other – not once, but all the time, for those feelings change as time goes by. There are thousands of other ways in which shame shows up between sexual intimates. We might keep our ideas about politics to ourselves, or our tastes in food or music – all because we are afraid of being rejected, or ridiculed, or ignored. One constant fear we all have is the simple fear of being different. That fear surfaces in an especially strong way in adolescence, as we look at various peer groups and feel their pressures and make decisions about which ones we will join. Are we "preppy," "punk," "mod," "jocks," "weirdos" or "brains"? Many daily decisions in the lives of teenagers are really identity-decisions. Decisions about how to dress, how to talk, how to wear their hair, what concerts to go to, what movies and TV programs to watch are agonizing. And why? Because these decisions show the world "who they are." And once "who they are" has been revealed, then "who they are" is open to ridicule, rejection, being ignored.

We were all teenagers once, and now know very well how much "identity decisions" continue through adult life. Peer pressure is not something that surfaces in adolescence and then disappears. It is a constant of human life. We are all constantly facing people who are different from us, in one way or another. We never meet anyone who is a clone of ourselves. And so, in every human relationship there is an on-going problem. How do we who are different get to be united in some appropriate way? The solution to the problem marks our transition into adult life. We have to know who we are, and value that as good even though it is different from what someone else is. And we have to discover who others are, and value that, even though it is different from what we are.

That is no small achievement. Thanks to our inborn shame, we tend to put ourselves down because we are different from others. Or else we put others down because they are different from ourselves. Or we might try to be more like others in order to win acceptance. Or we might condition our acceptance of others on their becoming more like us and meeting our standards. And one constant urge we all have is to conceal the selves that are so different. We keep ourselves to ourselves in order to protect them. We display false, pretended selves in the hope that these will be accepted, praised – in a word, loved. Shame is, at root, our fear that we are not lovable. Adam and Eve were ashamed of an action, their eating of the forbidden fruit. But that shame is a symbol for a deep shame that lives in the depths of every human heart: the shame that what we are, who we are, is unworthy, unlovable, and thus unloved.

This deep shame is really the root of a woman's desire to control her man (or a man's desire to control his woman). Another way to look at human relationships is to see them as power struggles. If I am afraid that my inner self is worthless and unlovable, I will try to get some sense of self-worth by controlling and manipulating my spouse. Then I will feel superior to him, and my sense of shame won't be so painful.

Do I want to visit my family instead of his for Christmas? If we are psychologically naked to each other, and not ashamed, I will try to tell my spouse about my preference. Also, I will tell him in a certain way. I will be honest and matter-of-fact, telling him how strong my preference is and what my reasons are. I will tell him in such a way that I am honestly open to negotiation on the issue, ready to listen to his feelings and take them into account. I will not try to manipulate him. I will not be afraid that he will manipulate me, reject me, or take advantage of me. And he will reveal his feelings with the same trust, the same vulnerability, the same willingness to negotiate. He will be naked to me psychologically, as I am to him. We will both be unashamed. The question of who will win, who is in control, "who's on top" simply won't arise.

The key to such vulnerability is passion. When desire flows freely between us – he drawn by my goodness, I drawn by his – we can't wear any psychological fig leaves. We don't need them. But let passion cool – his, or mine, or both – and suddenly, the need for control surfaces. Instead of feeling secure and loved, we feel unsure of our identities. We feel a need to keep control in order to protect ourselves. And we protect ourselves by treating our relationship as a power-play. Thus I might say, "Hold on. I can get my way on this if I play my cards right. I'll seduce him, right after supper." He, seeing my passionate advances, will be tense and wary – "Every time I let her get to me, she ends up the winner." He then restrains his passion, and the snowball has started to roll down the hill.

Shame, then, is the death of intimacy. Nakedness without shame is the only aura in which intimacy can grow, and that kind of nakedness is born of only one root in marriage: passion. People can be physically naked in a dispassionate way. Such is the way of exhibitionists and "macho show-offs." People can be physically clothed and yet, thanks to passion, psychologically naked. Such is the way of sacramental spouses. Their nakedness is their vulnerability. It is the trust by which each gives the other the free opportunity for control, confident that it won't be used.

Let's not get confused, now. Many a man who has fallen in love has blushed with a kind of shame, and told himself "I am not worthy of her." He compares his own goodness with the goodness of his beloved, sees that hers is much higher, and feels humility as a result. He feels almost a religious awe at her beauty, her goodness, and the fact that she loves him as much as he loves her. But that awe at someone's goodness and beauty, that blush of humility that leads a man to praise and thanksgiving, is not the shame which Adam and Eve felt after their disobedience. The embarrassment of the lover is a healthy, realistic response to the awesome mystery of human love and of human intimacy. A man stirred by passion cries out his unworthiness – but not because he is down on himself. The other kind of shame is false and the sign of a heart that is still centered on himself. But the "I am not worthy" of the passionate man is the cry of one whose heart has gone out to another and has been overwhelmed not by his own badness but by her goodness.

There is a world of difference, then, between shame and humility. The difference lies in where a lover's mind and heart are centered. The man who feels shame is, oddly enough, centered on himself. His mind is on himself, and his heart is, too. He looks to the one he loves for approval, for a shoring up of his own poor self-esteem. He is seeking to increase his own goodness rather than join ecstatically with the goodness of his beloved. That shame is the sign of the absence of passion. But the passionate man is forgetful of himself. His mind and heart are centered on his beloved. Her beauty and her goodness are all he thinks about – not what she can do for him, by way of approval. It doesn't occur to him to seek that approval. He nearly faints in awe at his good fortune, and the reality of an intimacy that he cannot doubt.

Very often the shamed, dispassionate man's words, "I am not worthy of her" have a bitter and resentful tone to them. Sometimes he even says what he really means by those words: "Who does she think she is? She's no better than I am. Why should I put myself out for her?" And that attitude is the death of intimacy – if indeed, it ever existed. The passionate man's humility and the dispassionate man's self-hate are not the same thing. They are exact opposites. And so are pride – the main fault of people whose passion is restrained – and the self-esteem of those who let desire lead them where it will. Passionate lovers are so secure in their own goodness that they completely forget about it. They have nothing to prove, no desire to prove themselves, and so their minds are filled with the goodness of their beloved. They let passion lead them where it will, into total self-abandon. Those who hold back their passion are anxious and afraid, centered on themselves as the most important person in the world. Their hearts are not abandoned to anyone else until they feel sure that their precious selves are safe from harm.

The author of Genesis, then, by showing us two people who hid themselves from each other in shame, was symbolizing something strong and deep in all of us: our self-primacy. We want to keep ourselves to ourselves, and for ourselves. And that desire is a protective device. We want to keep ourselves hidden from each other because we don't want our precious selves to be rejected. And we assume that they will be rejected because we fear that we are not good, not lovable, not worthy of even existing.

Remember when you were first in love? Remember how even little differences with your beloved caused you to flinch a little bit inside? Remember some little hesitancy to reveal your favorite kind of pizza, your fear that a certain hair style might not please? We laugh at teenagers in their anxiety to please, to wear exactly the right "uniform" of their peer group, to play the right records, and so on. But do we ever really get over that fear of being rejected? I still dread, for example, differences of opinion with my husband about our budget, or about permissions for our children. Both of us have learned over the years to discuss these things more openly than we once did. And nearly thirty years of living together in love have built an almost incredible trust between us that neither of us could have foreseen. But surprises still happen. Something will happen, we will have opposite reactions that are deep and strong, and both of us dread to let our reactions show. There is always the risk that this time – say, our firstborn's registration for the draft – the dialogue will not work, and we will have to live a long time with a painful open conflict between us. And the pain of having our opinions rejected always threatens to make us feel as if we are being rejected in our very selves.

The main focus of shame for any couple (and thus the area that most needs the healing brought by passion) is their intimacy itself, their relationship to each other. Shame about other areas of the self – moral principles, musical tastes, preferences in food and clothing – may seem like the focus. But really, the issue is always *us* – are we together or not? Are we dwelling, passionately, in each other's minds and hearts or not? For if we are, everything else is basically OK. "God's in His heaven, all's right with the world," as the poet says. Couples have found, in their passion, the balm that enables them to survive extreme tragedies (like the suicide, or murder, of a child). But if we're not, then everything else is basically askew. We may have a relationship that looks perfect on the surface. But if it is a brother-sister marriage, a congenial arrangement in which the flame of passion has died out, some very deep healing is needed. For in the desert of dispassion, the weed of shame will thrive.

How is it, then, with our passion? How intense is our desire? Those are the questions to be asked. The important point is not, "How do you like my new dress?" or "Aren't you proud of my latest promotion?" The important questions are, "How am I treating you as a person?" "Do you feel hurt when I say such-and-such?" "What are our sexual inhibitions? How shall we try to overcome them?" "Which plan for our vacation will give us the most time to cultivate our passion?" "What signs of selfishness do you see in me that I am not even aware of?" "How can I give you the maximum sexual pleasure?" "What kind of touching do you want from me tonight?" "How does that feel?" For the antidote to shame, the healing grace, is, for most people, the intimacy that is born of passion. And so, the main task is to cultivate that passion. Passion is the grace ˙which redeems us from the sin of Adam and Eve. Passion is the energy that turns shame into intimacy, that makes us psychologically naked before each other.

The nakedness that Adam and Eve shared before their disobedience is a symbol of the intimacy, the psychological nakedness without shame, that ought to be the ideal state of sexual couples. For the basic and ongoing problem of any human relationship is what we mentioned earlier: to face those who are different from ourselves, in love and acceptance. That love and acceptance require us to see ourselves as good, even though we are different from others, and others as good, even though they are different from ourselves. We need not put one down in order to affirm the other. But where, in all of human life, do we see a difference between people that is greater than what we find in people of the opposite sex? A man and a woman, no matter how similar they might be, are *more different* from each other than are any two men.

And in what circumstances do we find that difference, the sexual difference, more evident than when people are physically naked before each other? Clothes cover up precisely that part of us that is most strikingly different from our sexual opposites – the primary sexual features of our genital organs. And so, when a man and a woman are physically naked before each other, it is obvious to both that they are different from each other in some very important ways. When we have our clothes on, we can usually (though not always!) tell at a glance who is male and who is female. The new "unisex" style among young people sometimes makes that impossible. Men and women both wear jeans and T-shirts. Both wear their hair long. And don't we feel uncomfortable when we see someone – even a stranger on the street or subway – whose sexual identity is not immediately obvious?

The sexual identity of people is important to us. We want to know who is which sex, and we are uncomfortable when we do not know. Sexual identity is an important feature of every human being, and an important question in every encounter between human beings, even casual meetings of strangers who never expect to see each other again. A person's sexual identity is much more important than other features, like color of eyes, height and weight, even race. Our sexual identity is the most important fact about us, to ourselves and to each other. Usually people make their sexual identity obvious by the way they dress, but not always. When clothing does not give the label, secondary sexual characteristics give the necessary clues: obvious breast development or pregnancy tells us someone is a woman, even if she is wearing pants. And a mustache or beard, along with a deep voice, is a sure tip-off, no matter how long and elaborately styled his hair is.

When we think of the basic requirements of intimacy then, sex has to play a central role. The basic problem is how two separate and different people can become one with each other, in mutual respect and love, without ceasing to be two. We don't want couples to be clones of each other, with their sexual differences suppressed. We want those differences to be front and center, honored and cherished as central to the identities of the two spouses. And so, if you were going to write the book of Genesis – if you were going to compose a story that would symbolically contrast the ideal intimacy of spouses with what we usually find in our experience – what better symbol could you use than naked-ness? Shame – physical shame – is the best possible symbol for psychological shame, for the defensive hiding of oneself from another persons. Nakedness, by the same token – physical naked-ness – is the best possible symbol for the open revelation of our psychological differences to each other.

When we stand passionately naked before each other, we are saying, in a most powerful way, "Here I am, in my true identity, with nothing hidden, nothing between us, just you before me as I really am, and vice versa." We are admitting quite frankly that we are ready to let the magnet of sexual desire draw us together as quickly and as strongly as it can – and there is no more powerful magnet than one naked body to another naked body of the opposite sex. We are saying, as clearly as any human word, gesture, or action could possibly say, "Here I am, as the exact person that I am, ready to give my whole self to you and to accept your whole self in return." Two people who are psychologically naked before each other are already in a state of mutual, unres-trained self-abandon. Their self-abandon is the result of the passionate aura in which they live.

The writer of the story of Adam and Eve knew exactly what he was doing. He showed, as clearly as anyone could show, that there are two possible ways in which human beings can relate to each other. There is intimacy, in which we are "naked and not ashamed." And there is intimacy-avoidance, in which we hide ourselves from each other and from God because we are ashamed. Nakedness and shame, the two polar opposites. Sexual differences, the epitome of all human differences, is the most important difference of all. Sexual desire, the most powerful force known to human experience for drawing different people into a belonging to each other that respects, cherishes, affirms all those differences, including the most important one. Trust, self-esteem, self-abandon, total gift of attention and desire to another – all these elements of the various kinds of human intimacy are clearly and powerfully symbolized in this picture of sexual intimacy. The author of Genesis certainly knew what he was doing.

He knew what he was doing in some of the other details of the story, too. Why was Eve created? Adam was surrounded by all the glories of the physical world – the earth and the sun, the moon and the stars, the sky, the oceans, the plants and animals. But among all these there was no true companion for him. He needed someone like himself, for without such a fellow human being, he was alone. And that was no good. And so – God created, what? Another male to be his comrade? No. An angel or other spiritual being? No. Another animal, higher than the birds and fish and land animals? No. He created woman – another human being, but a sexual opposite. Someone basically the same, but different in one very important way – sexual identity. Sexual intimacy was to be the cure for Adam's loneliness.

And where was that fellow-human-yet-sexual-opposite to come from? Was God to take the slime of the earth once again and breathe life into it, so that the man and the woman could have the same origin? No, their closeness was to be even greater than that. They were not to be just two friends who came from the same hometown. They were to constitute a single, common self – not a "You and I" but a "We." What better way to symbolize such a common self than to have the woman taken from the man's body, his rib? There was the best possible reason for Adam to greet the woman as he did – that exultant cry of identification, "Bone of my bone and flesh of my flesh." What other words could say more clearly, "We are so close that we constitute a single self. All that I have, all that I am, belongs to you. And all that you are, all that you have, belongs to me." It's very easy to imagine, in fact, that Adam's cry came at the moment of the first human sexual act, the first orgasm.

The writer of Genesis was a literary and theological genius, indeed. For the symbolism he used in the contrasting part of the story is just as striking, and just as appropriate. Suppose you were writing the story, and you wanted to symbolize the rupture of that wonderful intimacy. How would you symbolize that two people, sexual opposites and thus capable of the deepest possible kind of personal unity, are instead divided from each other? How could you symbolize that their most important feature, their sexual identity, has become a focus of division between them? How would you symbolize their desire to avoid passion and suppress their sexual desire? How would you symbolize their desire to keep themselves to themselves, to hide their true selves from each other? How would you symbolize mistrust, self-contempt, self-primacy? How would you show, in a really striking symbol, the clinging to one's private self, the self-primacy by which we do not love each other but instead use and control each other for our own individual purposes?

One device for solving all these problems of choosing symbols would be to have the couple hide their sexual organs from each other, so that physical shame would indicate a deeper, psychological hiding of themselves from each other. And that is what the author of Genesis did: Adam and Eve made clothing for themselves out of fig leaves, thus covering up their primary sexual characteristics. With those characteristics hidden, the selves of which they were ashamed were somewhat protected. The power of sexual desire to draw them together was weakened and defused. The clothing said clearly,

> "OK., I'll give you part of myself. But the most important part is not to be abandoned to you. I'm withholding that until I'm sure I can trust you to see me as I really am. I want something between us, something I can hide behind. And I want something to insulate me from your true self, too."

And with the symbolism of their clothes comes Adam's famous statement making Eve the scapegoat for his own action. Why did he eat the forbidden fruit? "It was that woman you gave me." She is no longer the cherished bone of his bone and flesh of his flesh, but someone he looks down upon and uses. He is dishonest, blaming her for his own action. He makes her the source of the unhappiness that he brought on himself. He tries to shift the punishment that he deserves onto her – hardly the act of a man who loves his woman as he loves himself. Adam has shut off the force that had brought him to cherish Eve as his own body – his passion for her. With the death of passion, the death of intimacy ensues. What a powerful contrast between intimacy, as it is produced by passion, and the intimacy-avoidance that results from putting passion under wraps! It is the contrast between nakedness and shame.

Mike and Christine are a modern Adam and Eve. They are a real couple, but the story of their marriage is so typical that they are also symbols, as Adam and Eve are in the Bible. Mike and Christine fell hopelessly in love some years ago. As the song says, one enchanted evening, their eyes met across a crowded room, and passion was born. Throughout the months of their romance, they were totally absorbed in each other. They were so fascinated with each other that they could talk to, and listen to, each other all day long. They quivered with delight at each other's slightest touch. They stumbled over themselves trying to be kind and generous to each other. Sometimes they even quarrelled, or found themselves in a stalemate, because Mike wanted to do what would most please Christine, and she wanted to do what would most please Mike.

In their passion, they both found a clear and secure sexual identity. Mike had never felt so strongly what it is to be a man. And his joy in that identity was almost overwhelming. Christine felt the same joy in her secure and clear sense of being a woman. Their trust in each other – a trust that flowed from those secure identities – urged them to an eager sharing of every thought and feeling, every memory, every dream. Their love was a marvel to everyone who knew them.

When they began to make love regularly, their self-abandon was only intensified. Their loveplay was exuberant, exciting, and their desire carried over into their daily lives. They loved to talk about their love, to share memories about it, to fantasize their future passionate embraces. Thanks to sexual desire, they made a quantum leap out of the self-primacy they were born with. In just a short time – a few months – they found themselves far along the road that leads away from shame and into a complete psychological nakedness. They trusted each other completely, and found the urge to belong to each other a daily fact of their life together. In fact, they didn't even have to stop and think, or make decisions, about whether to give themselves to each other in all their day-to-day actions. The question never came up. Neither had a self to give, for they belonged to each other totally.

But gradually, little by little, a subtle change came over their relationship. Christine began to "run into walls" when she sought to know Mike's feelings. He seemed reluctant to talk about their relationship at times. He seemed more and more to clam up about his feelings. He didn't seem to want to share his days with her anymore. He seemed to tense up and clam up most quickly, and most firmly, when she could see that he was upset and would question him about his feelings. "It's nothing," he would say. "Don't worry about it." But Christine did worry about it. She didn't worry so much about Mike's problems – she didn't know what they were. But she did worry about his silence. Why did he no longer want to share his days with her? He used to rush home to the comfort of her arms after a bad day at work. Now he came home late, kissed her quickly, avoided her eyes, complained of being tired, and disappeared into his den until she called him to supper. Then he ate a quick, silent supper, and went back to his den. At bedtime, he undressed in the bathroom, turned out the light, and began to make love. But their lovemaking had changed, too. It was silent, hurried and tense, not very joyful. Mike had turned into a Silent Sam, in the bedroom and out.

Needless to say, Christine felt changes in herself too. One of her friends had a suggestion. The friend, Ginny, had found her husband suddenly very irritable, for no apparent reason. Everything Ginny said and did seemed to upset him. After several days, she finally asked him, "Have I inadvertently done something to offend you? Because if I have, I'd like to set it right." Tom, her husband, had replied, "No, darn it – I'm trying to stop smoking!" But that story didn't help Christine. Mike had never been a smoker. She began to wonder why he wouldn't confide in her anymore. Was there something wrong with her? Why didn't he trust her anymore? Why didn't he want to talk about "us" the way he used to? Why was he no longer honest and open about his feelings? Why was he pretending to be cheerful when he obviously was not? Why was he trying to hide an anger that was so evident to her?

It was no surprise that Christine's self-doubts began to affect her sexual feelings. She no longer thrilled at Mike's first touch, but found herself tensing up a bit. She certainly didn't want to refuse him her body, so she tried to be as cooperative as she could. But her passion was not what it used to be. She found it hard to warm up sexually because Mike was so distant from her in all their other contacts, especially in her efforts toward intimate conversation. Her somewhat dutiful, tense, "let's get this over with" lovemaking began to cool her passion even more. Before long, dispassion turned into real resentment. Christine made a compact in her own mind: "O.K., Buster. No passion for you until you give me your words. I'll be there for you in a minimal way, because I promised that in our wedding vows. But don't expect the enthusiasm I used to feel."

Needless to say, Mike was chagrined by her dutiful compliance. She didn't exactly refuse him her sexual favors. She was there, physically, and cooperative. But she no longer found him irresistable. In fact, it had been months since she had initiated any lovemaking. And her responses to his advances were quite restrained. Before long, he began to notice certain signals. Yes, she definitely was refusing him her body at times. She didn't come right out and say "No," but she indicated to him that he shouldn't even ask. For example, when he touched in that certain way that meant, "Let's do it," she would turn her back with some comment about what a busy day she had coming up tomorrow. Mike began to feel a deep, deep loneliness, a deeper loneliness than he ever felt before.

Mike and Christine soon found themselves in a downward spiral. The more Christine's passion cooled, the more lonely Mike felt. But the more lonely he felt, the less he felt like telling her about it. And the less he felt like telling her anything about any of his feelings. How could he hurt her by telling her how deeply she was hurting him? Better to just suffer in silence. And so, their intimate conversation almost disappeared from their life altogether. And as Mike got more and more lonely and withheld more and more of his feelings, Christine got more and more puzzled. She wondered more and more if there was something wrong with her, and Mike didn't entrust his heart to her the way he used to. With that puzzlement, she, too, began to feel a deep loneliness. And her passion faded more and more.

She no longer spent her days fantasizing their first warm embrace when he came home from work. It became harder and harder for her to warm up to him in bed. She began to find more and more reasons to show him, without saying so in words, that she didn't particularly enjoy making love. One day, she caught herself saying to herself,

"Why should I? He won't even talk to me. He doesn't treat me like a person anymore. He just wants me for my body. I'm going to ask for separate beds."

Pretty soon, both knew that a pattern had been set. Christine was making verbal intimacy a condition for sexual favors. Mike was refusing to meet that condition. And soon the two reached bottom. Mike began to withhold his sexual favors. He was impotent as well as silent. Nakedness had turned into shame. Both knew, and each knew that the other knew. But neither said anything. They simply said to themselves, "Well, this is how everyone said it would be, and they were right. We're lucky we had a few good years."

But what really happened to Mike and Christine? Had their marriage been a mistake? Was their dream of fifty years or more together, of a life of joyous sexual intimacy, an adolescent fantasy? Must they settle *for* what they have settled down to? In the words of the marriage counselor's column, can this marriage be saved? Does it need to be saved? Is it, in fact, the way things always are? Is it just what all of us should have expected?

To a secular mind, this marriage *is* just what is to be expected. That's how people are, and there's nothing we can do about it. Mike or Christine, or both, might find some renewed excitement with a new partner – a fling, perhaps, or a divorce and a new marriage. But that new excitement wouldn't last, either. Marriage hardly ever works out any better than this one. People are, after all, rugged individuals. They have to look for their own personal fulfillment in life. And the whole idea of lifelong commitment, and lifelong intimacy, goes against that. Marriage is a trap. They got themselves into it. Let them get themselves out.

But Mike and Christine are not secular-minded. They belong to a Church, whose members love each other as they love themselves. That Church – those loving people – have an enormous resource that secular society cannot even dream of. That resource is the healing grace of God. And one very powerful part of God's healing grace is the sexual intimacy that is so essential to the sacrament of matrimony. If Mike and Christine can once again surrender to that sacramental grace, they will experience a true sexual healing. And that healing will be no private matter. When it happens, Mike and Christine will assume a prophetic role in the

Church. Their renewed sexual intimacy will proclaim, loud and clear, to Church and world,

> God is Love,
> And he who
> Abides in love
> Abides in God,
> And God in him. (I John, 4:16)

QUESTIONS TO DISCUSS TOGETHER AS A COUPLE

1. What was your religious education like, especially in regard to sex?
2. What was your sex education like, especially in regard to religion?
3. Describe some specific ways in which falling in love improved your sense of being a man or a woman.
4. Give some examples from our popular culture of women controlling their men.
5. Give some examples from our popular culture of men who are models of "rugged individuals."
6. Give some examples from our popular culture of true sexual intimacy.

V

What You Say To A Naked Lady

M IKE and Christine don't have any deep-seated psychological problem. They don't have a troubled marriage.
They have a marriage that is good, stable, faithful, and basically
happy. But they have fallen into a pattern that is quite common in
such marriages: plain old garden-variety intimacy–avoidance. In a
way, their problem is a good sign. They are both afraid of deep
and total intimacy. But the reason they are afraid is that they once
experienced intimacy at some depth. Their original level of sexual
intimacy was quite high. And the vision of a deeper intimacy was
rather frightening. Mike and Christine were feeling the pressures
of their secular society, true enough. But mostly they were feeling
the inborn shame that is symbolized in Genesis as the result of
Adam's sin. That shame is precisely what Jesus, as the New
Adam, came to redeem them from.

What will that redemption consist in? The book of Genesis
gives us the clue. Once naked without shame, like Adam and Eve
in their original, ideal state, Mike and Christine are now ashamed
and not naked. The way to their healing, quite simply, is sex. And
their way to sexual healing is through nakedness – physical
nakedness as a symbol of psychological nakedness. But such
nakedness is a special kind of symbol. It is sacramental, a symbol
which *causes* what it symbolizes. Mike, of course, needs to become
much more open about his feelings. He needs verbal intimacy as
much as Christine does. In a way, his loneliness is of his own
making. He thinks it is due to the cooling of Christine's passion
for him, and, to some extent, it is. But her passion has cooled for a

reason – his withholding of his inner life, especially his feelings, from her. And so, Mike's loneliness is also of his own making. And what is of his making can also be of his healing. He needs only to cooperate with the grace that is already given, the grace of his sacrament.

Does he need to start confiding in his wife, then, telling her in long conversations about his secret terrors? No, that is not a realistic expectation. For the situation is not so simple. Christine, remember, is lonely too. Just as he needs to talk more openly to her, she needs to be more passionate in her desire for him. She needs a lusty sexual intimacy as much as he does. And so, her loneliness is of her own making, too. She blames it on Mike. If he hadn't clammed up, she wouldn't have felt mistrusted. And she began to withhold her sexual desire as a way of getting even for that mistrust. And so, Christine's loneliness is of her own making, too. And what is of her making can also be of her healing. Fortunately, the grace she needs is already given, too. She needs only to cooperate with it. But what will that cooperation be?

Does Christine need to approach Mike with lusty sexual advances, then? Should she trust the dynamite of sexual desire to blast him out of his clamshell? Hardly. For again, the situation is a bit more complex than that, and a bit more delicate. True, both of these lonely people are making themselves lonely. But they are reinforcing each other's loneliness, too. They don't have two parallel intimacy-avoidance games going. They have one rather intricate game, each one's moves toward shame and away from nakedness interwoven with the other's. Psychologically, Mike and Christine are dancing. They are both moving, and moving in the same direction. And their moves are intertwined, responsive to each other's. They are not doing separate dances in the wrong direction, but a tango, swirling down a dancefloor in each other's arms. Their sexual healing will have to be just as intricate. And it will be just as much a collaboration. Neither will find sexual healing without the other. They must continue their dance, but reverse its direction. How do they begin?

Sexual healing needs a technique. That is, spouses have to take some deliberate, carefully planned steps. They have to make decisions about where and when. And those decisions will affect many other decisions in their daily life. The first step is to agree to practice the technique. We call the technique "Skin-to-Skin Prime Time," or just "Prime Time," for short. It consists in just what the name says: devoting a minimum of thirty minutes of time each day to lying naked together in the privacy of their bedroom. And the time, as the name indicates, is not just any old time when they can fit it in. That is one common mistake of couples. They put off their intimacy until everything else is taken care of. And so, it usually happens late at night, when both are tired and already focusing on the agenda for the following day. Most couples don't even have any special, regularly scheduled intimacy time. That gets crowded out of their schedule altogether. And their neglect of lovemaking is definitely a sign of skewed priorities. Would any other important issue be left for the end of the day? What we consistently put off, what we leave for the time when our energy is at its lowest ebb, is what we consider to be the least important issue on our agenda. We shouldn't be surprised if desire declines when we constantly put other things ahead of it.

I can't complain that my identity has turned into that of Chief Cook and Bottle Washer if I insist on cooking and getting all the bottles washed before I will even think about sexual intimacy with my spouse. And my spouse – is he resentful about being treated as a mere money-machine? Maybe the reason that his identity has deteriorated is that we have both conspired, without realizing it. Do we habitually put off our time alone together until his work for the day is done? And does that usually turn out to be the end of the day, when we are both physically and emotionally exhausted? Then let's revise our schedule. What we do first is what we value the most. Our priorities are reflected in the way we spend our time.

Prime Time is not necessarily lovemaking time. But it is intimacy time. And, having put their sexual intimacy absolutely first on the list of their priorities, Mike and Christine will set aside Prime Time for it. Intimacy time will be the best part of their day, not the worst. The time of their sexual healing will be when both are at their best – relaxed and rested, free of distractions, sure that they won't be interrupted. And they will spend that time naked, Skin-to-Skin, communing with each other as deeply as they can.

Are we serious? Do we really recommend that Mike and Christine take thirty precious minutes out of every single day just to be alone, naked in each other's arms? Don't they need counselling? Don't they need to talk out their problems? Isn't good verbal communication the measure of a good marriage? Supose they do get together that way every day – won't they just end up making love in the same old way, only more often? If not, then why be naked? Why not just sit down together, or even lie side-by-side with their clothes on? And why make such a big deal of sexual intimacy? They are busy people, after all, with important things to do. Their "prime" time, the time when they are rested and relaxed, has to go to their children, their jobs, their house. They are lucky to get enough sleep three nights out of seven. Are they supposed to change their whole schedule, or what?

These questions, and many others that we could list, are all beside the point. For, yes, we are serious. We really do recommend Skin-to-Skin Prime Time – and not just for Mike and Christine and others who have fallen into their pattern. We recommend it for all couples. It is the best form of sexual healing we know of. But it is also the best form of prevention we can think of, too. A couple who practiced Prime Time from the day of their wedding would be unlikely to fall into the intimacy-avoidance dance that Mike and Christine are caught up in. For nakedness is the antidote to shame. Psychological nakedness frees us of psychological shame. But the most powerful way to psychological nakedness, for couples, is physical nakedness. Passion is the great power for sexual healing. And Prime Time takes the fullest possible advantage of the healing power of passion.

Let's follow Mike and Christine into their bedroom for their first session. Before they come to that point, they had had some fairly intimate conversation. Christine cannot *demand* verbal intimacy as a condition for sexual intimacy. She and Mike gave their bodies to each other long ago, and there is no longer any question about their being available to each other for sexual activity. And so, Christine, faithful to her vows, must give her fully passionate body to Mike, as he gives his to her. Her passion belongs to him, with no conditions, forever. It is not a reward for good behavior, but the living out of a promise.

And yet, she really needs the verbal intimacy that she cannot demand. She cannot be expected to warm up to a man who is unfaithful to her. And that is exactly what Mike is, in his refusal to share his feelings with her. He gave his body over to her at their wedding, too. And part of his body are his feelings and ideas, and the speech organs by which he shares those with his bride. He owes her the verbal intimacy she longs for, just as much as she owes him her passionate sexual desire. He must be faithful to his vows, too. That is not an optional matter. It is the keeping of a promise. It is his marital fidelity.

And so, the two must come to some sort of renewal of their wedding vows. They must repeat their promise to strive for maximum verbal and sexual intimacy, without making either one a precondition for the other. Both sex and conversation have to be set free from the restraints that Mike and Christine have put on them. But Prime Time is not a time for conversation, necessarily. Nor is it necessarily a time for making love. It might be either, or it might be both, on different occasions. But it can also be a very powerfully healing time of wordless, actionless communication. It can be a time of sexual intimacy that is beyond words and beyond actions. It can be the healing time which makes both sex and conversation more passionate. It can be a time of walking to the top of the mountain, every single day. Their first step is to agree to do it.

What will happen when man and wife, committed to renewing their romance, face each other, naked, with an uninterrupted half hour before them? What do you say to a naked lady? What does she say to you? How do you react to a naked, passionate, faithful man? How does he react to you? What you say to a naked lady is definitely different from what you say to anyone else. And so is what the naked lady says to you. In fact, the very nakedness itself speaks volumes. Spouses don't take their clothes off for anyone else in the whole world – at least not in the same way. I undress for my doctors, of course. And they touch and feel, poke and probe my most private parts – my sexual organs, my erogenous zones. But that nakedness does not establish an intimate relationship between us. If it did, my doctors would lose their professional standing – and rightly so!

But when I take my clothes off for my husband, and he takes his off for me, something special does happen. We uncover the unique relationship that we have with each other. That relationship is not a detached, professional one. It is erotic, intimate, and the basis of all our other associations with each other. When I meet my doctor socially (as I did once, at a parents' gathering at the school attended by both of our sons), our medical relationship is totally beside the point and we both know it. But when I am with my husband at a party or a meeting, what we are to each other when we are naked is basic, operative, and in the forefront of both of our minds.

What we say to each other in our nakedness is, then, different from what we say to anyone else. In fact, what we say to each other in our ongoing psychological nakedness is different, too. And that is just the point. Prime Time, with its physical nakedness, establishes an identity that we carry with us wherever we go.

When we embrace each other with nothing between us, we not only reveal ourselves to each other as sexual beings. We don't just say, "Yep! You're a man and I'm a woman, no mistake about it." That kind of clarity about our individual gender identities is important enough, and fun enough, too! But there is something else happening that is much more important.

That "something more" is the revealing and renewing of our sacramental, coupled identity. I don't just say, "I'm a woman and you're a man." I say, "I'm *your* woman and you are *my* man." And my husband's naked body says the same – "I'm *all* yours, precisely as I am, and you're all mine, precisely as you are." Mike and Christine, in their first session of Skin-to-Skin Prime Time, will be renewing their marriage vows. They will regain a clear image of who they are – not as individuals but as a couple. They will reinvest themselves in each other. The identities they have lost will be restored. Christine will no longer be, in either of their minds, Chief Cook and Bottle Washer. She will be Mike's passionately desired woman, Mike's passionately desirous lover. And Mike will not be, in his own mind or in hers, a breadwinner, identified in terms of his job. He will be a man, a very special man whose whole being is his passionate desire for Christine and hers for him. It is impossible for two people who are in love to ignore that fact, or keep it in the background, when they are naked in each other's arms.

More likely than not, Mike and Christine will be tempted to one of two things: irrelevant, distracting conversation or sexual intercourse. They will be eager to debrief each other, tell each other what they have been doing since their last meeting, make decisions about their children, share charming stories about their children and other people. But such conversation is a temptation that Mike and Christine must resist with all their might. It is a form of intimacy-avoidance. If they talk at all, they must talk about only one subject: themselves and their romance. And that talk must be carefully edited, too. Prime Time is not a time for settling grievances, for complaining, negotiating differences, and so on. It is a time for stimulating their desire for each other. They may reminisce about their past romantic times. They can share fantasies about their future passionate feelings. And they can – indeed, they must – share as openly and as spontaneously as possible their passionate feelings of the moment.

And won't they have such feelings to share! Just picture the scene: two happily married people, naked together in a privacy that they have arranged for the purpose, with nothing else in mind except the cultivation of the passion which once made them crazy about each other. What will happen? Surely, the two will embrace. One naked body is an irresistible magnet to another naked body of the opposite sex. It would be ridiculous, impossible to imagine, that they would sit in chairs across the room from each other and talk about their romantic feelings. In fact, we cannot even imagine them merely sitting side-by-side on the bed. They will hug and embrace. And why? Because there is a powerful symbolism in hugging, too. Hugging is a natural gesture for people who love each other. In a hug, we come as close together as we can without literally melting into each other. And in a naked embrace, we bring every possible inch of our own skin into contact with every possible inch of the other's skin. When two people wish to belong to each other totally, with nothing between them and no distance at all, the natural way to show that desire, and to act it out, is an embrace. So Mike and Christine will certainly embrace.

But we all know what that will lead to, don't we? Is there any possible follow-up to a naked embrace between passionate spouses besides sexual intercourse? Well, yes, as a matter of fact, there is. But even so, what's wrong with sexual intercourse? Given the avoidance game that Mike and Christine have been playing, there is probably quite a bit of pent-up desire for the sexual activity that has been refused and avoided over a long period of time. Probably many, if not most, couples do not make love as often as they need to in order to cultivate their sacramental passion. But that phase will pass.

Here again, we see how our secular culture can have a negative influence on people who hope for the joys of sacramental married life. In our culture, love is equated with sex, and sex is equated with intercourse. A "love story" is always a story about two people who are sexually attracted to each other. And sexual desire is only acted out in one way: through intercourse. Couples like Mike and Christine can be affected by these values. They may not even know about such glorious sexual intimacies as nongenital touching. Any touch is a prelude to intercourse – "Hey! If we're not going to do it, let's not even start." It's a simple law: sexual arousal must lead to intercourse. The idea of just enjoying that aroused state doesn't even occur to many couples.

Eventually, with practice, Prime Time will issue into some-thing else. What that something else will be, we cannot say. Once we allow passion its full sway, the future becomes unpredictable, and sexual intimacy varies from couple to couple, and even from day to day for the same couple. But all couples who have experienced it agree: there is a sexual intimacy which is beyond words and beyond actions. It is an awesome awareness of our presence to each other that leaves us staring at each other in silent amazement. The experience is something like what the mystics experience in their deepest moments of prayer, what others experience in perceiving the beauty of great masterpieces of art. In all these experiences, even breathing seems to be a distraction. No one wants to move a muscle, or speak or word. It is a supreme moment of realization.

For couples as for anyone else, daily life is a rhythm, a rhythm of realization. In the down-swings, everything becomes routine and ordinary. We take ourselves for granted. We take each other for granted. We take the beauties of nature for granted. We are never awestruck by anything. But in the upswings, we have a special, intense awareness of the beauty of many things. We get heightened insight into the mystery of our special persons. We are breathless at the sight of a sunset, or the sound of music. We are stopped in our tracks by a gospel verse that we have heard fifty times, and yet were never moved by before. Sexual intimacy follows this very same rhythm of realization. When a couple are first in love, they find each other literally breathtaking. Just the sight of each other is a joy so intense that they don't want to eat, can't sleep, don't notice what's going on around them. When they are alone together, they have many periods of silent contemplation. Just to be alone, hugging each other, is enough. They don't need to go anywhere or do anything. They don't even want to talk. Just being together is enough.

Prime Time is a technique for cultivating those special moments, this upward phase of realization. It is a way of deliberately creating that experience of intimacy every day, so that it doesn't get lost. It is a way of levelling out the peaks and valleys, so that the up-and-down rhythm doesn't happen. It is a way of turning the yo-yo into a constant, upward spiral. And it is a very effective way, because it uses the greatest energy known to man – the energy of sexual desire. There is only one way in which a couple can lose their realization, and that is through the decline of passion. And the logic works just as well in the opposite direction. There is only one way in which a couple can restore their lost realization, and that is through the stimulation of passion. For passion is what draws our attention away from ourselves toward the one we love.

Passion is the great force for breaking our fascination with ourselves, by making someone else even more fascinating. And so, it makes perfect sense to keep passion alive. For when we do, we keep our vision of each other alive. And we keep our intimacy alive as well.

Most couples are separated from each other for most of the waking hours of most of their days. One, or maybe both, will leave the family home in order to go to work. During those separations, their minds and wills will be turned toward something besides each other. They will be given over to their work, their children, and so on. The chances of losing their realization, their presence in each other's minds and hearts, are very high. The best way we know to restore their lost presence is through passion. And the best way to build passion is through Prime Time. And Prime Time should be scheduled as soon as possible, certainly within two hours of coming home from work. What can compete with seeing and touching the naked flesh of one's beloved as a reminder of what's important in their life together? Mike and Christine will find it pretty hard to think that their income is the most important thing in life, when they are locked in a half hour's naked embrace. They will find it pretty hard, while cuddling, to think in terms of who's right and who's wrong, or self-fulfillment, or "What am I getting out of this deal?" They will find it pretty hard to think, in quiet desperation, that life has no meaning, or that "No one really has a good marriage, anyway." They will find it hard to find ways of protecting themselves from each other's gaze.

And here the advantages of their nakedness are clear. The basic problem of human life is one that occurs in any meeting between two people, even brief ones. The problem is not always acute. Sometimes we don't even notice it. But it is always there. In order to achieve any kind of intimacy – which is what life is all about, after all – we have to solve that problem. It is the problem of how two different people can come together in unity of some kind without ceasing to be two. Adolescents feel the problem very severely, for the first time in their lives. But it is an ongoing problem of adult life, too. It is the problem of self-esteem, or, negatively, the problem of shame. It is the problem of facing someone who is different from ourselves, and seeing that person as good for being who he is. That sounds easy, but it isn't. What we usually do is put down one of the parties for being different. Thus, I put myself down, shame my self, because I think the other person is good, and I'm different, so I'm not good. Or else, I put the other person down, shame him or her, because I think I'm good, and the other is different from me, so he's not good. We can't both be good because we're different.

Modern psychology has brought this problem to light, but, really, it's the problem Adam and Eve faced in Genesis. Their nakedness is the key to that. What two people are more different from each other than a man and a woman? Sex is the greatest difference we know of. And when is that difference more evident than when we are naked before each other? When the author of Genesis tells us that Adam and Eve were naked and not ashamed, he is telling us a lot. They were very different from each other, fully aware of their difference, and yet cherished it. In their ideal state, before their disobedience to God, they saw themselves as good and saw each other as irresistibly good. And in that vision of two different goodnesses, they were drawn together in mutual love and intimacy. They were of one bone and one flesh. Their intimacy was total, and it was rooted in the maximum pressure point for intimacy: the naked confrontation of sexual opposites. Sexual intimacy which cannot pass that test is not genuine sexual intimacy. Sexual intimacy which can pass it, and does, is sacramental. It is the sacrament of matrimony.

When Christine and Mike meet for Prime Time, then, they are putting themselves in a very special situation. In their daily life together, they find many differences between them. They have different temperaments, different moods. They have different memories, different hopes. They differ in their perception of things ("Is it warm in here, or is it me?"; "Is the meat too salty?" "Hasn't this been a long week?"). In order to belong to each other, they have to find a way to mesh two personalities that are different in many ways. And in order to do that, they have to accept and affirm each other without putting themselves down. Mike is a man and sees the world from that point of view. Christine has a woman's view of things. Neither must shame the other, nor must they shame themselves.

When they were first in love, that was no problem. Thanks to passion, they felt an irresistible urgency to see things each other's way, to follow each other's preferences. He bored people with his constant quoting of Christine. She was an expert on anything and everything. She changed her taste in clothes, in music, in cars – all because of her desire for Mike. They treasured their differences, were fascinated by them. Now they find those differences irritating and boring. He has fallen back into his view of the world, and wonders "Why can't she see things my way for a change?" She has taken herself back to herself, and catches herself saying, "Why doesn't he just leave me alone? I've got things to do." Now, they are both lonely. And in their loneliness, they've begun to wonder whether they are really loved. They've questioned whether they are really lovable. They've fallen into the same shame that drove Adam and Eve to hide themselves from each other.

Self-esteem is a funny thing. Many people confuse it with pride, the pride that is one of the Seven Deadly Sins. But it isn't, really. Self-esteem is the what makes intimacy possible. Intimacy, remember, is the constant state of self-abandon. It is the constant state of self-forgetfulness. When we have it, we forget about ourselves and our self-fulfillment and our self-worth. Our attention is drawn away from ourselves toward the goodness of the ones we love. Our concern is drawn away from ourselves, too. It fades away in the light and heat of our devotion to the one we love. Self-esteem is the same thing as the "nakedness without shame" that symbolized the ideal human state in the story of Adam and Eve.

The other side of that coin is just as important. Many people equate humility with having a low opinion of oneself. The humble person, so they think, considers himself worthless, less good than others. But that isn't true, either. True humility is an honest recognition of our goodness and worth. It means recognizing our own special qualities, seeing these as good, being grateful for them and glad to have them. Humility is the same thing as self-esteem. Is it surprising that humility is essential for any kind of love, any kind of intimacy? The false humility, by which we consider ourselves worthless and unlovable, is not the way to intimacy. It is just the opposite – an obstacle. For false humility keeps our attention riveted right on ourselves. The person who feels that kind of shame is anxiously preoccupied with himself rather than with other people. He is not fascinated with the goodness of others. He looks at other people with an anxious concern for himself, wondering whether they are accepting or rejecting him, finding him lovable or not. He cannot enjoy intimacy because he cannot abandon himself to anyone else. He is self-centered.

People who play control-games have the same problem. When we get into a power-struggle with someone, we are constantly thinking about ourselves. We ask, "Who's winning, me or him?" "Who's going to end up on top this time? Didn't she win the last one?" We keep thinking about our own fulfillment, our own happiness, our own rights, what the other person owes us, and so on. Our attention and concern are centered inward, on ourselves, instead of being drawn outward by our beloved's goodness.

That self-centered shame is exactly what Mike and Christine are caught in. He withholds his feelings from her because to reveal them seems shameful. She restrains her passion because she is afraid to let herself go. Her sexual restraint deepens his shame, and his verbal restraint deepens hers. Skin-to-Skin Prime Time is the remedy for both. Prime Time will renew their passion, and with it will come flooding back the fascination with each other that they used to feel. Through the prism of passion, their vision will be once again corrected. Passion turns shame into self-esteem. And it does so in the most important way of all: a man whose wife obviously finds him irresistible feels loved, and lovable, precisely as a man. "My gosh, she sees me exactly as I am," says Mike to himself, "and she is crazy about what she sees. Whoopee!" Any self-doubts he might have had simply melt away. And that is true even about self-doubts that came from his job – say, a failure or a rejection which made him wonder about his worth as a person. How many times has Mike come home with his ego bruised, and felt it hurt even more deeply by Christine's signals that she can do quite well without him again tonight, thank you? But if he comes home knowing that soon he will hold her naked, quivering body in his arms for at least a half hour, the bruises he gets from the outside world won't seem so bad.

Christine's shame will melt away under the heat of passion, too. She has doubted her worth as a person because of Mike's failure to confide in her about his feelings. That silence has made her feel that Mike doesn't trust her, and then she has wondered what is wrong with her. She has felt unworthy as a person, too. What will Prime Time do for her kind of shame? Plenty! Can we imagine that a man, swept passionately into the naked embrace of a woman who finds him irresistible, will keep a clamp on his lips? Naked embraces have a kind of honesty about them that is almost impossible to escape. Christine will soon find that Mike can hardly wait to pour his heart out to her, even when that heart is wounded and bruised in its very core – his sense of masculinity. When a man turns his wife on sexually, and knows that he does, every single day, he will find it impossible to keep his joy to himself. And once joy is released, other feelings soon follow.

It may seem strange to our readers, but it is true: cultural values follow us into our bedrooms. What is operating in Mike and

Christine's marriage to cool down their passion and drive them back into their old shame is something bigger than them. It is a whole set of false ideas about masculinity and femininity, about what it is to be a man and what it is to be a woman. Mike and Christine have learned these false values so deeply that they may not even be aware of it. For example, it is a common myth in our society that men are not supposed to have certain feelings. And those are precisely the feelings that are necessary for sexual intimacy. Men are supposed to have no feelings at all except a simple, almost animalistic sexual desire – an urge that is satisfied by ejaculating. But they are not supposed to have more complex sexual feelings and needs like tenderness, sensitivity, vulnerability, a need to be comforted and praised. Rather than even wanting intimacy, they are supposed to "tough it out alone," to be "rugged individuals." And social acceptance is so important that a man who does not accept this "macho" image will suffer a lot. A man who really wants a deep intimacy will need a lot of support and understanding from his wife, and yet will scarcely be able to ask for it. He certainly won't get it from his buddies.

If Mike is to have a really intimate marriage, then, he will have to do a lot of unlearning. He will have to stop thinking that playing "Silent Sam" is the way to be a man. He will have to have the courage to resist his culture in the most difficult way of all – in his sense of what it is to be a man. In other words, he will have to risk being considered a "sissy" or a "wimp" by other men. If his friends and colleagues find out that he is working for a genuine intimacy with his wife, and that that is more important to him than his work, or his buddies, or anyone else, he is going to be vulnerable, indeed. They will not give him much support. They will want him to be a "rugged individual," but not in his individual way – only in theirs!

Skin-to-Skin Prime Time can be very scary for men, then. For in that situation, they are putting their manhood on the line in a most vulnerable way. Remember, Skin-to-Skin is a regular practice only after both spouses promise to give up the game they have been playing. Mike's game has been to starve his wife verbally, to deny her the verbal intimacy she needs by not talking about his feelings. In promising to give up that game, to share his feelings more openly in words, he has already taken a giant step in reversing his concept of what it is to be a man. That promise is an enormous compliment to Christine. And his meeting her for Prime Time is another compliment, one that is just as enormous.

For in meeting her for a half hour of naked communing, he is again making himself totally vulnerable to her.

But there is also an important vulnerability that is special to women. That vulnerability is also due to sheer physical differences in anatomy between men and women – the fear of pregnancy. That fear is a very powerful factor in many women, a force that dampens their enthusiasm for sexual activity and even for the intimacy experienced during Prime Time. Christine's passion is not, however, a simple physical fear. After all, there is a lot of discomfort and pain even in a normal pregnancy, and of course the risk that the pregnancy will not be normal. But for a couple who desire more children, that fear is rather easily handled. But there is another fear, one that is deeper and more powerful than that physical fear. And it is a much more formidable barrier to sexual intimacy between a couple. That fear is what we call "the fear of being a single parent."

Now, Christine doesn't fear being a single parent in the usual sense of that term. Mike is not going to leave her, or die, as a result of Prime Time. But they might end up with more children than they would have otherwise, and Christine doesn't exactly look forward to that. For you see, thanks to the pattern which they've established, she already is a single parent. Psychologically, the full burden of raising their children is falling on her. And she's not sure she can handle one or two more children "all by herself." Here, too, she and Mike have absorbed the myths of their culture, probably without even thinking about it. And that is another area in which they will have to be "in the world and not of it." For the myths and values of our secular culture in regard to childrearing have a powerful negative influence on the sexual intimacy of couples.

The same myths that make men emotionally simple, crude, tough, rugged individuals put women in charge of caring for children, especially when they are very small. Women once had no domain outside the home, and so, children were part of the home scene that women were in charge of. These myths are losing some of their credibility, thanks in part to the women's liberation movement. Now, when we go out to shopping malls or other places where there are crowds of people, we do see more and more men out in public with their babies and small children. We see men carrying their babies in Snugglies and pushing strollers. Sometimes their wives are not even along. More and more men are being employed in day-care centers and elementary schools.

Some corporations even allow "paternity leaves," so that new fathers can stay home for several months to care for their new babies and bond with them. All of these are steps in the right direction. They are good for fathers, good for babies, and good for the sexual intimacy of couples.

In fact, without an agreement that they will be fully involved with the raising of their children, husbands cannot expect their wives to enter wholeheartedly into a process of sexual healing. It's not just the hard physical labor involved in raising children that is at stake here. After all, many couples can afford to hire someone to do housework and laundry. But even couples with full-time hired help can find their passion inhibited by the wife's fear of being a single parent. What we need – what couples need for their own sexual healing – is a full partnership in the psychological process of raising children. And here is where the importance of verbal intimacy shows up again.

One very perceptive guest on a TV talk show remarked that "Children make their parents grow up much more than parents make their children grow up." He was absolutely right. For we don't really grow up until we work out, in intimacy with each other, our basic ideas about what it is to be a man, and what it is to be a woman. Along with that dialogue, we also need to work out, together, our basic religious beliefs – what we believe about God, the Church, morality. That dialogue is historical. It leads us to lovingly share the part of our lives that happened before we met each other. It leads us to share our sexual histories, our religious development, our sexual growth. And it forces us to make, in fear and trembling, many decisions about how to guide our children in their sexual and religious development. Any two spouses who really take part in that dialogue (especially if they have Prime Time as the focus of their life) will be doing the most important part of parenting together. And shared parenting will go a long way in releasing the passion of women for their men. A man, then, must give his woman all the verbal intimacy he can muster. He must share with her the ongoing sexual and religious dialogue of raising their children.

Any kind of intimacy requires vulnerability for all parties involved. But sexual intimacy makes men more vulnerable than women, simply because of the different anatomy of the two sexes. When Mike appears naked before Christine, his sexual response to her is obvious for both of them to see. There is no way in which a man can fake his feelings in that situation. If he has an erection, it is there, in all its glory, for both of them to see. And there is no way for him to pretend to have an erection when he doesn't. And so, he is vulnerable, indeed. In order for Prime Time to succeed (*not* for intercourse to happen, but for sexual communion to occur), he has to feel total trust for Christine. And she will have to prove worthy of that trust. She will have to give up her false ideas about what makes a man a man, ideas about sexual performance, about strength, initiative, and independence. She has to recognize the compliment Mike is paying her, and appreciate the manliness he shows in becoming vulnerable so that they can enjoy a true intimacy together. They must unlearn, together, some of the values that have been ingrained in them since their separate childhoods.

We don't want to underestimate the kind of vulnerability that Christine feels. But is it different. A woman can fake her sexual responses. Of course we don't recommend that. But just knowing that she could do so gives a woman a certain kind of security that is not possible to her man. She can pretend to be aroused when she is not, thus covering up what he might consider a sexual failure on her part. She can also be cool, withhold her passion, pretend not to be aroused when she really is. And that, too, gives her a kind of protection that her beloved cannot find for himself. Christine must not hide behind those false protections, however. She must come to Prime Time as naked psychologically as she is physically. And that will mean unlearning some of our cultural values about what it is to be a woman.

We can't be sure when it all started, but it is very possible that some myths about women's sexuality developed because of the ways in which women were oppressed in the larger, political and social world. When women were confined to the home, not allowed to have careers and other positions of power, or to control money, they very plausibly took charge of the home. The home became the woman's domain. She selected the house, did the decorating, and set the schedules for everyone who lived there. Part of that control was, naturally enough, control over the pattern of lovemaking between the spouses. She decided when, where, and even if. Such control was one of the few ways in which a woman could get any sense of being a person instead of a thing.

Myths about the psychological differences of the sexes grew along with these social arrangements. Women were thought of as intuitive, sensitive, with complex sexual feelings. They were good at human relationships and child-raising. Men, on the other hand, were seen as simple sexual creatures, needing regular ejaculation and nothing more. Men lacked the fine touch needed for intimate relationships. They were blunt, insensitive, needing a woman's hand to set limits on their sexual activity and thereby to tame them. Couple these myths with the idea that men, in order to be men, should conceal their feelings, and the stage is set for the pattern that Christine and Mike fell into without even realizing that they were doing so. Christine felt obliged to take charge of the home and to tame Mike's sexual appetite. The natural way for her to do that was to insist on verbal intimacy as the price he had to pay for sexual activity. "Gee, Father, it costs me three hours of conversation every time. By then, I'm out of the mood."

But in a way, history is beside the point. We don't need to figure out how it all began, or who is to blame for what. With Prime Time as our remedy, we can look at the here and now, and begin to change what needs to be changed. Christine and Mike are caught in an intricate psychological dance. They are dancing a parody, really, of a dance that can be truly intimate. What concrete changes can they look forward to as Prime Time teaches them a new direction, a new dance-tune, and some new steps for following that tune? To put it bluntly, which is more important, sex or conversation? Who changes first, Mute Mike or Cool Christine?

Actually, the question is a mistaken one, and a concern about what happens first will keep our couple locked in their present dance. Spouses are human beings. And human beings are, as the philosophers say, a strange kind of inbetween critter. We're animals with bodies and feelings like other animals. And so, we need passion. But we're not *just* animals – we're intelligent, users of language. And so, we need words, too. Verbal intimacy and sexual intimacy: we need them both. And neither can come first, really. Mike and Christine have to change together, both at the same time. And they have to let each other do so. Neither can say, "I won't change until he does (or she does)."

What they need to do, actually – and this is exactly what Prime Time will do for them – is to get back the passion they felt when they first fell in love. Christine didn't hold back her feelings then, waiting to be satisfied verbally before she would get passionate. She lived in a permanent state of sexual arousal and loved it. Those were delicious feelings! And Mike – did he stop and think before he spoke, wondering whether he'd be trapped by a scheming female if he let her know his feelings? Hardly! Words came easy to him, just as passion did to her. Trust was automatic. And trust is what they need to renew. Passion will show them the way.

The first step in renewing their trust is taken when they agree to Prime Time – at least to a trial period of, say, 90 days. But that agreement should include a promise to be more open verbally about their feelings. A daily love letter, perhaps, to put their fantasies into words. Without some efforts toward verbal intimacy, Prime Time will just be more of what they already have. It will turn into a ritual for going to bed. It will be the same old mechanical, wordless lovemaking that leaves both of them lonely afterwards. Mike will continue to turn his back afterwards, wondering why his ejaculations leave him feeling lonely. Christine will continue to lie beside his snoring body, bewildered and wondering why he doesn't trust her. But sexual intimacy cannot wait very long. Certainly the two cannot put off the practice of Prime Time until they acquire the skills of an adequate verbal communication. And it will take time for them to learn the gentle art of nongenital touching, of silent communion, and yes, of spoken verbal intimacy.

Prime Time does not aim at sexual intercourse. But it will, very likely, increase a couple's frequency, at least for a while. That frequency is not a bad thing. In fact, our experience on this point has been very interesting. And it confirms our view about the basic problems that underlie the decline of passion. It also confirms our belief in Skin-to-Skin Prime Time as a technique of sexual healing. That experience is as follows: when Prime Time is first proposed to couples, women are somewhat hesitant about it, while men can hardly wait to get started. But after couples practice it for a while, those reactions completely reverse themselves. Women become enthusiastic, while their men begin to draw back.

The reason is the same in both cases, namely the way in which all of us have limited the possibilities of sexual intimacy by equating it with sexual intercourse. Women are suspicious of Prime Time at first because it sounds like more of the same wordless, mechanical sexual activity that they dread. They are afraid that their lonely feelings, feelings caused by their own control games, are going to get worse. They are also afraid that the husbands who want them only for their bodies will use them as sex objects if they allow their passion its free release. But their husbands are eager for Prime Time because to them it sounds like "Catch-up" time, a chance to make up for the sexual activity that their wives have been holding back. And for a while, maybe it is.

Eventually, though, the pressure of real sexual intimacy comes to the fore. Almost without their realizing it, couples learn the possibilities of nongenital touching and nonverbal communication. Mike's desire for sexual release yields its place to his awe at Christine's beauty. Her body, quivering at his slightest touch, becomes almost transparent. Little features he had never noticed before – a catch in her breath, the widening of her eyes – leave him awestruck and amazed. Christine's desire to talk goes out the window as her trust in Mike gradually returns. The wild self-abandon that she has been bottling up is suddenly released. And then, nature takes its course. The healing power of sexual desire begins to do its work.

One big surprise awaits them, though. As the possibility of greater intimacy opens up, so does the possibility of greater vulnerability. For those two go together. Soon Mike may feel that all this new sexual frequency is not as good as he thought. It's leading him down a path that he didn't foresee – the path to vulnerability toward, and dependence on, a woman. He finds himself dependent on Christine for his very identity as a man. And now that he has dropped his guard, he is more afraid than ever of coming under her control. That new fear of being manipulated through his sexual feelings is a moment of genuine crisis for their intimacy.

Fortunately, the remedy for Mike's fear of intimacy is built right into intimacy itself. For both Mike and Christine are finding their entire life transformed by their half hour of Prime Time. Paradoxically, just as Christine relaxes her demand for verbal intimacy (because she is finding something better), Mike is feeling an urgency to give it. Just as their new trust allows her to relax in their lovemaking, it allows him to relax in their conversation. It's funny – both sex and conversation become easier once we see that we can give up our demands for them. The wordless, actionless communion of genuine sexual intimacy makes both words and actions easier, and even delightful.

Actually, what is happening to this blessed couple is a perfect experience of God's healing grace as it was described long ago by St. Augustine: "Something that is done in us, without us." Mike and Christine are not just getting some psychological benefits. They don't come out of the bedroom just feeling better, with tensions relieved and egos massaged. The change in them is much deeper than that, and one which they cannot manipulate by any kind of gimmick. Sexual intimacy is a gift that cannot be

contrived or created by any human effort. All we can do is create
the conditions in which we can, and will, accept the gift which
God, in His mercy, will give us.

But Prime Time does create those conditions. If Christine
and Mike have the courage to persevere, to accept the ever-
growing vulnerability that comes with ever-deepening intimacy,
they can expect certain results. Those results will be a very exact
parallel to the features of the declining passion that we described
earlier. In other words, the wounds that need to be healed – the
various elements of shame – are exactly the ones that will be
healed.

The most important element of sexual healing that will result
from Prime Time will be ever more clear, and more secure, sexual
identities. Even as they act against the stereotypes of our culture
and give up false ideas about what it is to be a man, and what it is
to be a woman, intimate couples will get a clear vision about what
it is to be sexual. He will feel manly in an entirely new way, and
her femininity will blossom. The self-doubts and false humility
that once locked them into their shame will disappear. They won't
be so afraid to reveal themselves to each other. They won't
suppress their differences out of a fear of hurting each other's
feelings, either.

They will, to use Fran's words about the death of her husband,
experience the end of the world. Their private, singles' world will
end. But they will survive. They will come through the experience
of dying to self, and see that life goes on. They will see that it not
only goes on, but is beautiful. They will see what Jesus saw in His
death and resurrection: Death to self is not a loss, but a gain. The
life that goes on after death, and is beautiful, is not grief and fear,
but joy – joy in a new and deeper intimacy.

Prime Time is, quite literally a foretaste of Heaven. And it
gradually transforms all of our time together, so that all of our
time becomes Prime. It is the power of passion that does that.
Passion is a strong healing force. If we give it a chance, it builds
our mutual trust. A man becomes totally vulnerable to his woman
because he cannot resist her charms, and doesn't want to. And
when he puts his very manhood on the line in perfect trust, her
passion becomes a fireball. In the heat of such passion, who could
hold back his words? Both find themselves babbling, like the
Apostles did on Pentecost.

So, what do you say to a naked lady? Everything you can, fella.
Everything you can.

QUESTIONS TO DISCUSS TOGETHER AS A COUPLE

1. Which is more important to a sacramental marriage, sex or conversation? Why?
2. How would a decision to practice Skin-to-Skin Prime Time lead a couple to clarify the priorities of their time together?
3. How does physical nakedness lead to psychological nakedness?
4. How, besides talking or making love, might a couple spend their Prime Time?
5. Describe some of the specific ways in which Prime Time heals shame.

VI

You Never Walk Alone

C HRISTINE was surprised at first, when Mike mentioned her control over their sexual activity, and how that gave him a general sense of frustration and loneliness. In fact, she used to joke about it. People would ask how many children she had, and she would say, "Four – a 10-year-old, a 7-year old, a 2-year-old, and Mike, age 33." Mike didn't think it was funny. He felt like one of the children, one of the "things" in Christine's world that she arranged to suit herself – like a piece of furniture, almost. But she didn't see his point at first. Wasn't that the way it was supposed to be?

"Besides," she said, "I never say 'No' – or at least, only when it's right."

"You don't have to," said Mike. "Your other signals are clear enough. It seems that every time I look forward to some extra lovemaking, you make sure it doesn't happen. You suddenly get busy. Or you pick a fight. Worst of all is when you do what you did last night. You were there for me, but just barely. You were cold and matter-of-fact, as if you could take me or leave me alone."

"Well, what did you expect! You left me hanging all day, waiting for you to call from work. How can we make love when we're not even friends?"

But Christine did finally see that she was using a veto power over her sexual activity with Mike. She also saw how her inhibiting her passion for Mike, making it conditional on his verbal intimacy, was a flaw in their sexual intimacy. But she had been acting with the best of intentions. She had assumed control of the household, including the bedroom, because that is what she thought a woman was supposed to do. But once she became aware of her control pattern, then she had another problem: she didn't know exactly how to change something so deep. She had to find a way to be "friends" with Mike all the time. For her attitude really did permeate their whole life together. What was she to do? Prime Time was the answer to her question. It was a way to keep their intimacy intact, even when there were unresolved grievances between them.

With their 30 minutes of naked communing every day, Christine found even that deep attitude changing. Instead of saying, "We have to talk about this before we can get together," she soon said, "We have to be sure we're together before we can talk about this." And Prime Time became their way of being sure they were together – together all the time.

Even her tone of voice changed. Before, when Mike failed to call her, he was met with a tense and stony silence. Supper was hasty and matter-of-fact. Once the children were settled for the night, he and Christine would also go to bed. And finally he'd hear her resentful, accusing question: "Why didn't you call me? I waited all day for nothing." He'd mumble a quick apology, turn his back, and go to sleep. But now, when he didn't call, she knew he had a good reason, and didn't pressure him to explain. She greeted him with a lusty kiss, a warm embrace, and everything arranged for Prime Time. "Sally's coming to watch the kids and give them their supper. We'll have a whole hour alone. Too busy to call me today? Well, you'll be glad to relax. Come with me."

At first the thought was a little scary. It is never easy to give up control, and Christine saw her schedule, her sense of being in charge, her sense of being a person, going down the drain, as Prime Time took her out of herself more and more. But she took the risk. Mike had made it clear to her that he was not interested only in her body. He wanted verbal intimacy, too, and was ready to work for it. And so, she began once again to trust his lovemaking as an act of tender passion. With that trust, she relaxed in his arms for half an hour every day. Both let their feelings flow freely. Both were surprised at how they could read each other's body language. Mike's words poured out, too. But mostly, the two of them were exicted by little signals they had never paid much attention to before. Eyes that widen in surprised delight, muscles that quiver at a slight touch, smiles that cannot be repressed speak volumes. But let's hear Christine's own words, as she described the experience to a group of trusted friends:

> "It is much more than looking at your sexual activity and increasing that. It is saying 'Yes' to being involved in a sexual relationship that is a whole way of life. It means communicating to each other, 'You are my life.' And you know, something happens to me when I let myself be filled with Mike. When we are really communicating in our sexual relationship all day long, I really don't give a damn if the dishes get done, and I don't care about my checklist. It changes my whole personality. At first I didn't want to change, and sometimes now I don't want to, either. I don't want to be filled with Mike. I'd rather be filled with Christine. But that is changing, more and more."

Mike noticed the changes, of course. He was the center of her life once again. He no longer lived in "her" house, as one of the children. He was a man, and he knew it. In fact, he had never felt so virile before. Even their children noticed the difference. Once in a while, Christine would fall back into her old control game. Mike would stiffen and resist. Soon the whole atmosphere of the house would be tense. And then a little child would lead them:

> "Why don't you two go to your room for a while? You seem pretty crabby. I'll do the dishes and answer the telephone."

Meanwhile, Mike was changing too. He learned new verbal skills. He began to recognize his different feelings, and put them into words for Christine. But he did much more than learn a new language. He changed his whole idea of what it is to be a man. In fact, he did more than that: he changed his whole way of *being* a man. It took a long time. He made a lot of mistakes. He often failed, and fell back into his old Silent Sam role. But he kept trying again. Christine was really patient with him, and gave him lots of credit for his good intentions. But that came easy to her, thanks to passion. For Mike was giving her his very self. He was laying down his life for her, as surely as if he had rushed into a burning building to save her. And she was laying down her life for him. There was no doubt that she was the treasure of his heart. And he was the treasure of hers.

We are not exaggerating when we say that the transition to genuine sexual intimacy is a way of giving up our lives for each other. When a woman whose passion has become inhibited over a period of years gives herself up to the Prime Time experience, she undergoes a kind of death and resurrection, too. A sacramental marriage is a constant process of giving up our lives for our friends

– for those passionately loved friends, our spouses. It doesn't happen overnight. We take two steps forward and one back, and then four or five forward and three back, and so on. Changing behavior is hard enough for human beings. Changing attitudes is even harder. And changing identities is hardest of all. In fact, we have to wonder if it would ever happen, for the ordinary run of people, without the energy of sexual desire behind it.

But it does happen. And that is what is awesome. Constancy is handed to us on our wedding day in the form of a down payment. But the rest of it comes gradually over the years. What happens is that our moments of realization get stretched out. They come more often, and last longer. But realization is twofold in a sacramental life. When we realize our sexual intimacy, we are doing two things. One is what people usually mean when they speak of realizing something. "Now I realize what you meant the first time you said 'I want to be all yours!'" We realize the awesome unity that passion brings. That is, we recognize it. We know it, are aware of it, in a special way. It is vividly real in our perceptions.

Thus, Mike and Christine cry out, or whisper, "I always knew that you loved me, but now I realize how true that is!" But realization is something even more wonderful than a new perception. It is a new reality. To realize our sexual intimacy is to make it real in a way that it's never been real before. I often call my husband Pygmalion, after the hero in the Greek myth who made a statue of a beautiful woman. He fell in love with its beauty. And behold! The statue became real under the power of Venus, the goddess of love. That is what happens to passionate spouses. Passion produces something new in both of them, a new power to love, a new intimacy. When we marry, we are all somewhat like Pygmalion's statue – cold, hard, lifeless stone. But the heat of passion breathes life into us. The cold, hard marble of our hearts comes to life as we learn to love in ways that we didn't even know we could.

I often reflect on the kind of person I was in my adolescence. I wasn't all that different from other adolescents, both of my own generation and every other generation. If I had to put it in one word, I suppose I would say "self-centered." I was interested mainly in myself, and thought about other people only in terms of how they related to me. I didn't even think of them as persons with feelings and sensitivities. In that respect, I was insensitive. And that was especially true of my relationship with boys. I cringe now when I remember some of the insensitive things I did and said. One memory is particularly sharp. Three couples, six of us, had gone to a movie, and were headed for a nearby restaurant afterwards for something to eat. We were all relatively poor college students, and it was taken for granted that we would have something small and inexpensive – a hamburger and a Coke, probably. But as we settled into our seats and looked at the menu, I thought it would be a fine joke on my date to pretend I was going to order the most expensive thing on the menu. So, I said, "Oh! I think I am going to order the T-Bone steak." To this day I remember, with regret, the panic in the eyes of my date and the stiffness of his whole body as he sat beside me the rest of the evening. I had embarrassed him.

Of course such insensitivity is typical of adolescents, especially in dating activities. A very complicated game is usually played. The kids pretend not to like someone they like, for fear of scaring that person away, of "coming on too strong." And, at the same time, they pretend to like someone that they don't like, just so they will have a date and not feel left out. They are really using each other, though without realizing it. Rarely do teenagers have genuine intimacy with each other. They seldom form friendships with members of the opposite sex that involve honest exchanges of ideas and feelings. They seldom meet each other on any deep personal level.

The reason, of course, is that teenagers are too insecure. They haven't found themselves yet. They haven't discovered "who they are" and they are confused by their rapidly changing feelings and ideas. One day they are in love, and the next day they hate each other. One day, this girl wants to be a psychiatrist, and the next day a cocktail waitress. They are deeply afraid of exposing their true selves to each other. Basically, they don't even know what their true selves are. But even when they do – or think they do – they are so afraid of not being accepted that they keep those true selves under wraps. They play constant defensive games with each other. They build themselves up by putting each other down.

Our inborn self-primacy and shame reach a kind of psychological high point in adolescence. Psychologists refer to it as the "adolescent identity crisis." It is like the crisis in a physical illness – the point at which the disease reaches its maximum strength. After that, the patient is either going to get well or die. In psychological growth, when we reach an identity-crisis, our shame has reached a kind of new high point. And we must do one of two things in

order to get out of the crisis: we either convert ourselves to the
kind of love for others that makes intimacy possible, or else we
remain in the deep shame and self-primacy that seal us even more
deeply into our loneliness.

The way out of the adolescent identity crisis, in the eyes of
contemporary psychologists, is to move from narcissism to
altruism, from self-primacy to love for others. It is the same move
that we saw earlier, the one that happens when people fall in love.
In fact, that experience is the most common one for moving
people out of their adolescent self-primacy into tender devotion,
out of shame into intimacy. We have to wonder if most people
would ever make that move without the energy of sexual desire to
get them started.

One line from the famous "Peace Prayer" of St. Francis says it
all: "Lord, grant that I may not so much seek to be loved, as to
love." That sentence does not just describe perfectly the process of
becoming an adult, of psychological maturing. It captures the
essence of the redemptive process which all Christians are to
undergo. Our whole spiritual life, including the sacramental life of
the Church, aims at teaching us, and empowering us, to seek to
love rather than to be loved. And that is a real turnaround, a
conversion. When President Kennedy said, in that famous line of
his inaugural speech, "Ask not what your country can do for you.
Ask what you can do for your country," he was asking for the
deepest change that human beings can make. He was asking us to
accept the heart transplant that Jeremiah spoke of. For most of us,
the chief sacrament for turning us around is the sacrament of
matrimony. And the heart and soul of matrimony is the ongoing
sexual intimacy that gradually becomes our whole way of life. If
we practice Skin-to-Skin Prime Time, then we ought to see some
long-lasting effects. We don't want to come out of the bedroom
with just the temporary effects of a psychological Jacuzzi. Feeling
better is not the point – or, at least, not the main point. What
might some of those long-term effects be?

It seems surprising to some people, but it is true: one of the
main effects of Prime Time is to tenderize our hearts. I really hurt
the boy I was with when I joked about ordering a steak. I scared
him, embarrassed him, deepened his shame. After some years of
passionate intimacy with Ed, I now know better. I am less
thoughtless, more careful of everybody's sensibilities. Of course I
fail many times, every day, and do carelessly hurt peoples'
feelings. But I do it much less often than I used to. Now I

sometimes stop and think before I speak. I've pretty well given up an old habit of sarcastic teasing – and all because I realized, in light of our passion for each other, that such teasing was hurtful to the one I love. And I also saw how it was hurtful to other people, too. Now, when I make a sarcastic remark to someone, it is usually because I've let my passion for Ed cool temporarily. And that cooling down of desire throws me back into my adolescent insecurity and shame. It causes me to seek to be loved rather than to love.

Sex has a real tenderizing power. Often, people think of sex as just the opposite. To some, it seems more like a brutalizing, gross animal instinct that needs to be suppressed and tamed. Sometimes, of course, it is that. But not for couples who are in love. When people have real sexual intimacy, sex is just as lusty and energetic. But the energy makes them soft and tender – not just toward each other, but toward everyone they know. The passion between me and Ed has given me a whole new view of how to order from a menu, for example. Sometimes it is important to consider prices, and to do that with some tact and delicacy. Money matters generally lie very close to peoples' self-esteem. Sometimes it's OK to order the most expensive items, sometimes it's not. Sometimes it's OK to joke about prices, and sometimes it's not. It all depends on circumstances, whom we are with, and so on. That is just one example, in one area of life, where I've developed a sensitivity that I didn't have before sexual intimacy became something of a way of life.

The change began dramatically enough. Before we fell in love, I had just discovered my talents for teaching philosophy. With great excitement – looking toward a lifetime of the teaching that I loved – I applied for opportunities for further study and teaching. Such interesting possibilities were open – I could study in such adventuresome cities as Toronto, Washington, New York, even Rome or Paris. As a single person, I was free to live wherever I wanted, to do whatever I wanted. The possibilities were thrilling!

But all of that changed in the twinkling of an eye – or of four eyes. As soon as Ed and I knew that we were in love, there was no question as to where I would live – a place I had never even considered, Milwaukee, Wisconsin. My plans for an exciting teaching position, or an opportunity to study, were suddenly totally unimportant (though both eventually worked out). Once we began our life together, I made many more changes. Ed needed a low fat, low cholesterol diet. That meant changing something very basic to any human being – my eating habits. A changed menu meant learning new cooking skills and revising shopping patterns. It meant changing our food budget, and then other areas of our budget. It meant many conversations about our priorities, and thus about our identities.

But the point is, passion made all of these changes so urgent that I actually enjoyed making them. This was my new life, as Ed's wife, and I loved meeting each day's revelation of what that was going to be. And the biggest change of all would never have been possible without our mutual desire. Ed chose, as his life's work, to be a professor in a Catholic university. That meant a relatively low salary for our entire life – about ⅓ of what he might have earned with his business skills. Of course that decision forced many others. It didn't mean poverty, but it did mean never having a luxurious home, not taking trips to Europe every summer, not having a comfortable security for our old age. It has affected our children's lives, too, in countless ways.

But being a professor was our agreed upon way for him to lovingly put his talents at the service of the Church. Only passion could have led me to support that decision, and to make all the sacrifices that it has led to over the years. Passion, in fact, made them easy. It has been my way of assuming an identity, as Ed's wife, that has seemed so obvious and right that I don't even think of sacrifices as sacrifices. They are the warp and woof of our being *us*, and *us* is what both of us desire to be, more than anything else we can think of.

Do sacrifices ever seem irksome or difficult? Do I ever regret getting into our financial situation? Yes – and precisely when my passion for Ed cools, and I lose the selective vision that focusses on his goodness as the unique person that he is. When he becomes just another one of the people in my life, I soon find myself in competition with him, seeking my share, my rights, my control. I wonder, angrily, why can't it be my way for a change? In fact, my whole mood, my sense of who I am, changes so that other people and their needs become irksome, too. Life becomes irksome, I become irksome to myself.

The way out of that mood is, invariably, a new stimulation of my sexual desire for Ed. So, I invite him to an extra Skin-to-Skin session. Then I look for an understanding priest and go to confession. I confess as my main sin that I have let my passion decline. What is my purpose of amendment? To renew my passion as the focus of my life. It means devising, along with my confessor, a penance that will renew my passion – perhaps reading a chapter of the Song of Songs, perhaps going for a long walk and reminiscing about our early love.

But the most important step is also the hardest. It is the hardest because I know it will work, and I don't always want it to. It is scary because I also know that it will work in some way that I don't exactly foresee. And so, it is a big step into the unknown. That step is to ask Ed to join me in praying for renewed passion, preferably at the Kiss of Peace at a liturgy.

Many couples think that, when we go to mass, we should leave our sexual feelings at home. The liturgy is a time and place of hushed, restrained, solemn "spirituality." We shouldn't look at each other, let alone touch! Actually, though, the liturgy is the high point of unity for all present, unity with each other, and unity of the Church with her divine Bridegroom. The passion of couples, then, should be at its height during the Mass. And it ought to be obvious to everyone present. It ought to be obvious not only in the way that spouses give each other the Kiss of Peace. It should also be obvious in the way that couples greet other people in the congregation. For their passion for each other ought to tenderize their hearts toward everyone in the Church. And tender hearts don't show themselves in limp, distracted, mechanical handshakes.

Once our prayer for passion is answered, the other healing effects become obvious once again. For example, trust is renewed. There is a proverb, the line of a song, which, like all other proverbs, has a kernel of truth to it: "You always hurt the one you love, the one you shouldn't hurt at all." Partly that statement is true because we live in close quarters, and so there are many more chances to say and do the hurtful things. Another factor, of course, is that the one we love trusts us, and so is more vulnerable to us. We can hurt the one we love more deeply than we can hurt others who don't give us the same trust and vulnerability. But passion has a wonderful, healing effect on these hurts. That is part of its tenderizing power. As passionate spouses develop a greater sensitivity, they hurt each less often. "Hey! That's one of my sore spots. Please don't ever say that again." "Oh! I'm sorry – I didn't know that. Of course I won't do it again." And I don't. The hurts are less frequent. And the ones that do slip out are easily and quickly forgiven. It's easy to forgive someone you trust. And it's easy to trust someone you are crazy about, and who is crazy about you.

Here's a point that young people miss when they "move in

together," under the illusion that they can "try out" their sexual relationship without the commitment of marriage." "Isn't it better," they ask, "to find our first whether we can live together? It's just good divorce prevention." Their mistake is in thinking that you can "try out" sexual intimacy on a temporary, conditional basis. When two people live together in a sexual relationship, they are bound to hurt each other in many ways. No two human beings can associate closely without many conflicts, clashes and hurts. But without a permanent, ongoing sexual intimacy that they deliberately cultivate, they never develop the trust that makes it easy to forgive. When we're not committed to each other, we have to hold our passion in check. And then it cannot have its healing effect. And it has to be held in check as long as the two make no commitment to a permanent sexual intimacy. For when we let it go, it naturally leads us to self-abandon. Isn't it true that when people want sexual activity without any strings, they have to say so? That's because the strings are built in. Passion is a glue between people, not a wall.

It is true, then, that "You always hurt the one you love." But there's another side to that coin. We don't have a proverb to express it. But it's true, just the same. There's also a special healing for the hurts that lovers inflict on each other. Passion is the balm for those hurts. It's a special, marital form of that great Christian virtue – mercy. That tenderizing balm carries over, too, into other relationshps. It's common, for example, for children to give their parents a lot of hurt and pain. That is especially true when they are adolescents. In order to become adults, adolescents have to separate themselves somehow, from the two people who most make them feel like children. Those two are, of course, their parents. But most adolescents are quite clumsy about managing that separation. They don't have the skills of communication and intimacy. Thus my son, for example, will tell me that I am a stupid person when I ask his help with some electronic gadget that he knows more about than I do. It hurts to be called stupid to my face, and adolescent boys don't have healing skills, either. They are awkward in expressing affection, even while they feel it. But I have another, sure-fire source for the healing of hurts inflicted by my son – my son's father. When we meet at special times to savor our sexual intimacy, those hurts just seem to fade. And then I face my son with tenderness rather than resentment. He'll learn, and I'll find ways to teach him. Meanwhile I treasure him as the offspring of our desire for each other.

When we are on fire with sexual desire, we see the good points in all people and overlook the bad. And that is especially true for those special people who are the offspring of our desire. Our spouse's faults seem cute, in fact, and we easily forgive them even when they reappear in our children. When passion is dormant, we will say, in an exasperated tone of voice, "Look at this mess in your room. You're just like your father." But if we keep passion alive, those words have an entirely different ring to them. "Isn't he cute? He's just like his father!" In fact, the mechanism of heredity is quite mysterious and beautiful. When we can appreciate its beauty, we are in awe of the power, wisdom and love that created the world. Can you believe that just the sight of a child's peculiar way of walking, or the curve of his nose, can be a religious experience? It can – for a passionate woman who sees that child as a replica of her tenderly cherished beloved.

Betty put it rather well one day:

> "When my mind and heart are full of Al, I go around with this big smile, snapping my fingers and humming. And it's awfully hard to scold the kids when I'm humming and snapping my fingers."

She sees them through rose–colored glasses. Her glasses are the prism of passion, which she and Al have nourished in their daily Prime Time. In past years, they had often confessed the sin of being impatient with their children. And they prayed for patience everyday. But then they found something better – passion. When we deliberately keep our passion alive, we don't even need patience. We have something better. With passion, we see our children differently. They don't look like exasperating little duties and obligations, burdens to be borne in patience. Of course we correct and discipline them. Any loving parent does that. But Betty and Al, and all passionate spouses, do it by praise rather than criticism. And that method isn't just more pleasant for everyone in the home. It is effective. Our teenagers, for example, will acquire the skills of dialogue much more quickly if we show them how to disagree without being disagreeable. And then, if we reinforce their progress by praising it, they will learn even more quickly. Instead of telling us we are stupid, they will someday learn to say, "These ground rules look different to me. Can we talk about it?"

One of the skills we all need for any kind of intimacy is the skill of being a good listener. We need to become good listeners ourselves. We also need to teach our children how to be good listeners. But what are those skills? Precisely the ones that come naturally to a passionate spouse. A good listener gives full attention to the one speaking. He doesn't let his attention wander. He keeps eye contact, and doesn't fidget. He doesn't interrupt, or change the subject. And when the speaker finishes, the good listener says something to the point, something that shows he has heard and tried to understand. Those interior attitudes are part of being "naked and not ashamed," "self-forgetful," "self-abandoning." The good listener gives up his self-primacy and gives his attention over to his beloved.

But when a couple meet daily for Prime Time, they don't even have to try to be good listeners. Their attention is automatically drawn away from themselves and onto each other. Their desire leads them to forget themselves. A man face-to-face with the love of his life, naked and quivering with anticipation, isn't about to change the subject, interrupt her, or mull over what he is going to say as soon as she is finished. He is utterly fascinated with her, his attention riveted on her. Under the heat of passion, all the attitudes that keep us from being good listeners melt away. We are healed of our insecurity, our self-righteousness, our pride and our anxiety. When we're naked together, we listen to each other. It is impossible to do anything else. But the habits of good listening gradually seep into the rest of our life together, too. And by our example, we can help our teenagers learn how to be good listeners. Gradually, they will come to see that you don't have to be hostile to someone in order to be independent of them.

Another one of the most important results of Prime Time and the intimacy that it builds is the transformation of anger. Anger is a major problem in just about everybody's life. And there is a lot of confusion around about anger. Two contradictory views are held. One view, the one I learned in the Church as a teenager, is that anger is a sin. In fact, it is an especially terrible sin. It is one of the Seven Capital sins – those that lead to many other sins as well. Anger, I remember, leads to contention and murder, among other things. And so, I used to confess the sin of anger, X number of times, every week. And every week, I would resolve once again not to become angry, and perform a penance to make up for my past sins of anger.

Later in life, I learned another view of anger. I learned there are two kinds of anger, one good and one bad. I learned that the kind I had felt in my adolescence was a healthy anger, one justified by my situation. And I learned that it was unhealthy to suppress that kind of anger, as I had been doing for many years. In fact, I should have acted it out very forcefully, so that someone would have noticed me and given me the help I needed. One big healing that I have experienced in my sexual intimacy with Ed has been in this area. It took many years, and is not a complete healing yet. But passion can definitely help us here. The tenderizing of our hearts can lead us to feel and express healthy anger in ways that build intimacy instead of tearing it down.

The basic idea is that there is always some time-lag between our feeling angry, our recognizing that feeling, and our expressing it in a truthful and loving way. The healthier we are, the shorter that time-lag is. The ideal is to recognize anger as soon as we feel it, to know that we are angry and why. But very often, we can feel angry – for days, maybe, or even years – and not know it, or know it and not know exactly what we are angry about. As our anger is transformed by sexual healing, we find that we become aware of it more quickly, and identify its source almost immediately. Once we have that awareness, we can then find the right way to express the anger. And when we become really healed, really skilled at building intimacy in all our human contacts, the expression of all feelings becomes easy and almost automatic. We can learn to be forceful without being hostile, and to tell the right person what we are displeased about and why. We can also negotiate with that person the change we would like to see, and then work together to bring it about. That kind of anger, and that way of expressing it, builds intimacy rather than tearing it down. And passion makes that possible. Without passion, we look for revenge when someone displeases us. But when we're tenderized by desire, displeasure becomes a time of bringing hearts into closer unity.

For example, I used to feel a pretty strong anger when I would come home from a hard day of teaching – perhaps after a night class – and find the sink full of dirty dishes. I wouldn't say anything. I would just do a sullen, slow burn. Everyone around me would know that I was displeased about something. But they didn't know what it was. Consequently, they didn't know what to do to make things right. And so, they wouldn't say anything, either. There would be a sullen silence in the house for a day or so, until my bad feelings gradually dissipated. But the issue was never resolved, only suppressed. And so, the anger was there, ready to surface again when I came upon the next sink full of dirty dishes. And it gradually got more and more intense.

One day, I decided to look at this situation in the light of my sexual desire for Ed, and my affection for our children. In the glow of that intimacy, I realized that the dirty dishes upset me because they aroused an old and deep insecurity that I had acquired in my early life. I took the dirty dishes as a sign that nobody loved me, that nobody spent their evening thinking, "Now, how can I make Mom feel good when she comes home?" They had other things on their minds! Moreover, their view of our house was different from mine. To me, the house was Responsibility with a capital R. It was my duty to prove my worth as a person by doing all the household chores. And yet, I couldn't. There simply wasn't enough time in a day to cultivate our sexual intimacy, care for two lively, active teenagers, meet the daily demands of my profession, and keep all the household chores up to date. Something had to give!

But what? The way I had been handling my anger was slighting my passion for my husband, and with it, my affection for my children. My sullen suppressed rage was darkening the whole atmosphere of our home. My insecurity and exaggerated sense of responsibility were chasing passion out the window. It's pretty hard to warm up sexually when you're biting your tongue so as not to say, "Don't you love me enough to do that dinky pile of dishes?" (One wonders why, if the issue was so dinky, I was making it so big.) Anger drives sexual desire out the window.

But sexual desire drives anger out the window, too. Once I realized that I was angry, and what I was angry about, I was able – thanks to passion – to put things in better perspective. The dirty dishes, no longer the symbol of an imagined personal rejection, did not loom so large in my mind. I began to apply at home something that I try to teach all my students – that we shouldn't *feel* responsible for things that we cannot *be* responsible for. I felt less guilty about housekeeping chores that didn't get done when I was teaching. And most importantly, as I basked in the glow of renewed sexual desire, I realized that my family was not engaged in some sort of conspiracy to make me unhappy. The dishes were left, not because they didn't care about my feelings, but because they felt secure and comfortable enough, in *their* home, to enjoy their interests – TV and reading, telephone calls to friends – without false guilt feelings over unimportant things. And then I saw that the security with which they relaxed and enjoyed their home was a very obvious tribute to the sexual intimacy that created that atmosphere. The cloud of suppressed anger began to lift.

I still don't like finding dirty dishes in the sink when I come home from a long, hard day at the university. Passion doesn't lead us to gloss over differences, to hide our feelings of displeasure or pretend that they don't exist. Differences are unavoidable wherever two or three are gathered together in anyone's name! Intimacy does not consist in avoiding conflicts, but in resolving them. But what makes that resolution possible and even easy is sexual desire. Passionate spouses have plenty of disagreements and conflicts, issues between them that have to be discussed and settled. But their style of conflict-resolution does not inflict angry wounds on each other from a vantage point of wounded pride and self-righteousness. Rather, they learn to speak their anger tenderly, with a view to making a treasured intimacy even deeper. They open negotiations with a genuine desire to be flexible and find a solution that will please everyone involved.

Why is it that, when a spouse opens a conversation with the phrase, "We have to talk," the other almost always cringes inside? Somehow the talking we "have to" do is never intimate, never passionate or tender. It is always angry, self-righteous, accusatory. It's never about how precious we are to each other, how desirous we are of each other, but how one of us is right in some conflict or other, and the other is wrong. We know that it is anger speaking, but not passion, when we hear such phrases as "I am going to be honest with you," or, "It's a matter of principle." More often than not these are the phrases of the anger that is seeking revenge. They contain a stubborn self-seeking and a wish to hurt the other person. The one who speaks them is interested only in resolving his or her own bad feelings, and thus is using the spouse in order to feel better. That is the approach of the anger which is a capital sin. And it is the exact opposite of the anger which is an aid to intimacy.

The healthy, intimacy-building way to express anger is the way that passion suggests to us. A passionate couple will not try to avoid their conflicts. But their first step in resolving them is to make sure that their passion for each other is intact. They have total rights to each other's bodies for the sake of love, after all. And their tongues are part of those bodies. St. James even said,

> "Among all the parts of the body, the tongue is a whole wicked world in itself; it infects the whole body. . . . The only man who could reach perfection would be someone who never said anything wrong." (JA 3:2-6).

Now there is a high standard! But that's what our wedding vows commit us to. Many people take for granted that it is an accepted pattern for spouses to speak sharply to each other, and critically of each other. They think it is expected practice to complain, to correct each other, even in public. Some couples that you overhear on the bus seem to live in a constant state of understated hostility. They sound angry even when they don't mean to be – talking about the weather, for example! Many couples are more open about their conflicts than they are about their passion. They brag about "getting things out in the open." But those "things" are always angry things, not passionate ones.

Prime Time can heal that pattern, too. The way in which passionate couples resolve their conflicts is quite different from what we have just seen. The first step is to make sure that their intimacy is intact. A session of Skin-to-Skin is the best approach. Such couples cherish their intimacy above all else. Certainly they don't jeopardize it by standing on their rights and demanding justice. They hang onto their marital identity at all costs. For only passion gives them a right to speak out, to negotiate some change in their way of living together. To put it figuratively, couples whose passion is dormant make their marital identities episodic as a result. They are not always spouses to each other, but only from time to time, when their passion is sporadically aroused. And so, when they have a conflict to resolve, they put the problem between them and face each other in an angry confrontation. But in that posture, as they attack the problem, they also attack each other. A passionate couple, on the other hand, maintain their marital identity all the time. They live in an aura of desire. And so, when they have a conflict to resolve, they are side-by-side, with the problem out in front of them. Instead of attacking each other, they face the problem together. And in resolving it, they come to be closer than they were before.

Take my sink full of dirty dishes as an example again. Does that seem like a trivial matter to use as an illustration of the making or breaking of sexual intimacy? It is not. There's no such thing as a trivial conflict in an intimate marriage. Issues are not what they seem to be on the surface – dirty dishes, for example. They are always, just below the surface, about "us." The real conflict is always over our perceptions of each other, our love for each other, our trust in each other's love. And the soil in which our trust and love find their nourishment is passion. Keep that alive, and its fruits will follow. Let that die, and you may win a lot of battles.

But you will have lost the war against the anger that is a capital sin.

When stony hearts are turned to flesh by the warmth of desire, the words of St. Paul are written on them: "Be slow to anger, and quick to forgive." Passionate spouses are not afraid to lose points in an argument. Their life together has only one point – passion. What fosters that is what both really want. They don't exaggerate minor displeasures into raging tantrums. They are careful about their timing, willing to sleep on a problem, to put it in writing, to wait for the right moment to bring it up. When my passion is dead, thanks to my own failure to cultivate it, I can make a total war out of a sink full of dirty dishes. "Why do I have to do everything around here? Doesn't anyone else care? What's the matter with me? What's the matter with you? Why have I failed to teach my children any better than this? You all know how upset it makes me to come home to a dirty kitchen – you must be doing this on purpose." And so on. But when I see things in the perspective of passion, I can calmly ask, "Is there some special reason why nobody did the dishes tonight?" And usually, there is. When there isn't, it's been a case of simple forgetting, because everyone was absorbed in something else. They were relaxed, and enjoying their passionate home, without the anxieties that can be imposed by an insecure mother.

Passionate spouses, then, come to something better than conflict-resolution. Conflict-resolution is a blessing in itself, and not to be minimized. But negotiations of differences can bring something deeper – a genuine reconciliation. An intimate couple can be in a furious verbal fight, suddenly catch each other's eyes, and melt on the spot. Then, they fall into each other's arms, and the issue fades in the warmth of their desire for each other. Later on, they'll tell friends the story of their fight, and find that what was once a painful conflict has become a joke to them. When the husband tells the story, he emphasizes his fault, whereas during the fight he saw only hers. And the wife makes the same reversal. They forget the motes in each other's eyes and see the beams in their own.

Try to picture our coming together for a Skin-to-Skin session when I am angry about the dirty dishes. We both take our clothes off. We are drawn like magnets to each other's naked bodies, and are soon locked in an embrace. Thanks to this total, all-senses, experience of closeness, I find my anger almost immediately defused. In fact, if I tried to keep a self-righteous distance, I would feel ridiculous. Anger requires distance, but distance is practically impossible to two naked lovers. It almost seems a requirement for self-righteousness to have our clothes on. It is hard to keep our mind on the issue before us when we are face-to-face in our nudity. And that, of course, is precisely the point. What am I going to do and say as I see my husband's obvious response to my naked body, and feel my response to his? After all, I'm not a voyeur, and neither is he. And we're not exhibitionists, either. Our physical nakedness is not a distant, dispassionate display. It's a sign of, and a step toward, a deeper, psychological nakedness. Its an act of belonging, not of using each other. So what do I do? I become instantly vulnerable, and find my anger defused. "What was it I was going to tell him about my hurt feelings? How was I going to get my way, and show him that I can hurt him as much as he hurts me?" It's really hard to remember. I can't nurse my anger, because I'm not dressed for the occasion. Nudity just isn't the right costume for seeking revenge.

When protective clothes come off, then, so do protective attitudes. And there is nothing more poignant, more touching, than the vulnerability of a naked, passionate spouse. Soon the memories of past moments of sexual intimacy come flooding back, and with them the changed perception, the corrected vision that the prism of passion supplies. Once again, we see each other as we really are. He's not my enemy, thoughtless of my wishes, out to get me with a dirty kitchen! Prime Time is great preventive medicine for sexual intimacy. For just as those who nurse their anger cannot belong to each other, so also those who belong to each other cannot nurse their anger. The two attitudes are completely contradictory.

When a passionate couple experience some kind of conflict – the issue can be anything – they will always have good news for each other, and bad news. Their approach should be to tell the good news first. That good news is always the same, their ongoing passion for each other. And the best way to tell it is Skin-to-Skin. Marital communication is pore-to-pore, not mouth-to-ear. (We almost titled this chapter "*Pore ad pore loquitur.*") When we give the good news first, the bad news – that there is some negotiable difference between us – doesn't seem so bad. It doesn't seem so bad, because it really isn't. For what is really important is also constantly true – our belonging to each other in passionate desire.

There is a simple test couples can use to decide whether a

discussion has been truly marital, truly sacramental or not. The test is not, "Did we make the right decision?" And it certainly is not, "Did I get him (or her) to see my point?" It is not even, "Was that pleasant and agreeable?" Too often when people say "That was a good talk," they mean that they won the argument. "I enjoyed that" too often means, "I got my feelings of my chest." All of these evaluations are self-seeking. They indicate a lack of passion and sexual intimacy. Clearing the decks does do that – it clears the decks. But it doesn't usually deepen our belonging to each other. The test of a truly marital conversation is always the same: Did we meet in passionate self-abandon or not? If we did, then, no matter what decision comes out of the discussion, it has been a "good" conversation – good for passion, good for intimacy, good for desire. And if we didn't, then it hasn't been good for anything.

It all comes down to a question of identities. If a couple are to have a fully sacramental marriage, then they have to give first priority to their sexual intimacy. Passion is more important than their jobs, their social status, even their children. Their marriage is not just the most important fact of their life. It is what makes all the other facts important. Sacramental spouses find their identities in their belonging to each other, and not in their work or other social roles. They don't marry casually. They don't set themselves a scenario in which they get their education first, get settled into a good career, and then look around for someone that will fit their "lifestyle." They prepare more carefully for marriage than they do for their life work. Their marriage is not just one of the things that they do. It is the center of all else, an identity which they constantly live and cultivate. They are like the pig in the story of the ecumenical pig and the ecumenical chicken. The chicken suggested an ecumenical breakfast of ham and eggs. "No thanks," said the pig. "For you, that would be a contribution, but for me, it's a total commitment." For sacramental couples, passion is a total commitment.

Take a clue from the business world. The really successful men and women of that world are totally dedicated. They have a single-minded devotion to making money. They don't just avoid what is harmful or settle for mediocre success. They don't brush off a period of lost profits with a resigned sigh, "Oh, well. You win some and you lose some. There's always tomorrow." A devoted businessman has more drive than that. He takes every small step that he can to increase his profits, knowing that those small steps add up over time. He makes the most of every opportunity, and does so with gusto and enthusiasm.

Couples cannot do anything less. Half-hearted desire won't do. Neither will episodic passion. We have to watch for every slightest chance to deepen our passion, taking every small step that we can. And if we do, we'll find the story of Adam and Eve reversed in our own lives. It isn't good for a man to be alone, and it isn't good for a woman, either. In our Easter Vigil liturgy, we call Adam's sin a "Happy Fault," because it brought us our Redeemer. And our life in Christ is even better than what Adam and Eve had before their sin.

For sacramental couples, that new, redeemed life is the life of sexual intimacy. Thanks to the healing power of passion, we can enjoy a truly awesome intimacy, one that is even better than what Adam felt when he called Eve "flesh of my flesh, and bone of my bone." That something better is the sacrament of matrimony – "A great sacrament, in Christ and the Church."

QUESTIONS TO DISCUSS TOGETHER AS A COUPLE

1. What are some of the typical ways that women exercise veto power over their sexual relationship with their husbands?
2. What are some of the typical ways that men withhold verbal intimacy from their wives?
3. What are some typical changes that come about when a woman gives up her veto power?
4. What are some typical changes that come about when a man becomes more intimate verbally with his wife?
5. How does passion heal anger?

VII

All the World
Loves a Lover

REMEMBER the quiz we presented back in Chapter IV, about naming the most spiritual couple you know, the most passionate couple and so on? Well, it's time now to add another question: Name the most *apostolic* couple you know. Describe them: are they very conscious of their membership in the Church? Are they active parishioners? Do they keep up on the world news? Can they be counted on to contribute to starving Ethiopian babies? Do they really want to spread the gospel, the Good News of Christian salvation to all the world? If so – fine. But there is one more crucial question: Are they, or are they not, the same couple we have already been describing – spiritual, morally good, and passionate? Is passion the main element of their unity? If so, we've got a sacramental couple.

In marriages that are luminously sacramental, prophetic passion is their way of being holy and morally good. And so, for such couples, sexual desire, spiritual life, and evangelization all come together. They are not separate compartments of life. Just as prayer is not one compartment of a contemplative life but a constant state, so also passion is a whole way of life. It is not just an occasional event, but the aura in which we live. And that aura is also our spiritual life. It is, in fact, our prayer. It is also our prophecy, our way of preaching the gospel and building the Church.

People do not usually connect sex with spirituality. And that is because they do not usually connect body and soul. Anything to do with the body and our interaction with the physical world is connected with our "lower" selves – our physical urges and animal appetites. But spiritual things are the opposite, so they say. Our spiritual life is that part of us that we give to praying, going to Church, reading religious books and magazines, making retreats, doing works of charity. Despite a lot of improvement in attitudes about sex in the Church, there is still a lingering sense that it is, if not evil, somewhat less desirable than more "spiritual" realities. In the words of Dory Previn's marvelous song, "High is right, and low is wrong." And *high* means spiritual, while sex and other bodily matters are "low."

What do we have to do, then, to heal this split between sex and spirituality? For that healing will then be prophetic in the Church. Our ideal, after all, is not a couple billing and cooing in the corner while the world collapses in disaster all around them. Our ideal is to build the Church of Christ. We are co-operating, in our passion, with Jesus' prayer that *all* might be one.

The way to begin is to get back to some of the basics of our religious beliefs. Do we believe that God created heaven and earth, or don't we? Genesis doesn't say that He made heaven good and earth bad. No, He saw everything that He had made, including human sexuality, and "saw that it was very good." Do we believe in the Incarnation, or don't we? Do we believe that Jesus really became a man? The heresy that He only appeared that way was condemned a long time ago. He really was human, incarnate, bodily. In fact, he still is. Don't we believe in the Resurrection of Jesus? He didn't just use a body for a short time, to accomplish His mission on earth, and then go back to heaven as a spirit. No, Jesus died, rose again to bodily life, and ascended into heaven in bodily form, as a man.

In one of the most moving homilies I have ever heard (it was on an Ascension Thursday), our pastor mentioned a recent experience he had had in our neighborhood supermarket. A mother, shopping with a small child, was quite impatient because the child was dawdling. She jerked him rather roughly, two or three times, and ordered him, in a stern voice, to stay close to her. She lifted him by one arm and dragged him down an aisle. She was not unusually upset. It was obvious that this was her normal way of handling the child – as it is for many people. But, our pastor observed, if we realized how precious those little bodies are, we could never manhandle them. If we could just realize that our bodies, and those of our children, are going to live forever, imbued with the grace of God, we would show them an awed gentleness.

We would touch each other, and our children, with the soft caresses that lovers use in the most awesome moments of their passion. After all, do we believe in our own resurrection from the dead, or don't we?

When we are told, then, to be "in the world but not of it," we are not being told to look down on our bodies and the actions – and the passion – associated with them. Whatever our spirituality is, it has to include our bodily selves, and our existence as part of the world of nature. We are supposed to be as deeply immersed in that world as we can possibly be, so that God can redeem it along with us. Thomas Aquinas, the great theologian of the thirteenth century, has a very helpful idea here. When he wonders about what our risen bodies will be like, he insists that they will really be material bodies. They will not be mirages. And yet they will be spiritualized. Now, what in the world is a spiritualized body? Not a ghost, or a mirage, he says. It is a material body which is utterly, completely, under the control and domination of our spirit. And our spirit, in its turn, will be utterly and completely under the control and domination of the Spirit of Christ, Who is the third person of the Trinity.

Now, partly what that means is that our bodies will not be subject to the pains and sufferings caused by material forces in this life. We will not die or get sick; we won't feel the pangs of hunger and thirst. But what is more important is that every single action we perform, and every iota of passion and emotion that we feel, will be what fits with our loving response to the Holy Spirit. And the Holy Spirit is the love of God poured forth in our hearts. Our spiritualized bodies, then, will be perfect expressions of the same spiritual life that we live now – except that that spiritual life will be much more perfect, deeper and purer. And what is our spiritual life now? It is the life of love. It is the life in which we love God with our whole hearts and souls, and our neighbors as ourselves. For sacramental couples, the source and center of that life of love is our sexual desire. So, sexual desire is our spiritual life now. And sexual desire will spiritualize our bodies in the life of resurrection which is to come. It will energize our love for all the other people who make up the Communion of Saints.

Being "in the world and not of it" is no easy trick, however. For being immersed in the world means living very closely with other people, including those not sharing our beliefs, and yet not accepting their secular values. We certainly live in a secular age and a secular culture. The life-goals held up as ideals in our culture are those of a world "come of age," a world in which "God is dead." The mature, sophisticated, modern person no longer believes in such quaint medieval notions of God and life after death. And the quaintest, most out-of-date notion of all is that marriage is a sacrament of salvation. Indeed, the notion of marriage proposed in this book would simply be laughed out of court by sophisticated moderns. They believe and live by the myths about sex and romance that are so common in our cuture. Those myths – especially the myth that passion should decline, that men are rugged individuals, and that intimacy is a woman's game – are part of the world that we must not be of, that we must not give our hearts to. We have to be spiritual, not secular.

How, then, do we put sex and spirituality together? How can it be that the sexiest couple we know is also the most spiritual, and vice versa? How can we combine a passionate life with one that is morally good? How does holiness make us more passionate? And how does passion become prophetic? These are important questions. The sexual healing that is our theme is not just a kind of therapy that makes us feel better about ourselves. That sort of healing can be the height of selfishness, and thus the opposite of the spiritual life that we live in the Church. It can be what one author called a form of idolatry, "the cult of self-worship." No, the sexual healing that passionate couples experience is much deeper than that. It is a healing of our self-primacy. It is a healing of our reluctance to belong to anyone except ourselves. It is a healing of the shame, the psychological shame, that is symbolized by physical shame in the Adam and Eve story. It is nothing less than the indwelling of the Holy Spirit, "the love of God poured forth in our hearts." Sexual healing is a form of belonging – first to each other, then to the Church, then to the whole world.

The key to all of Catholic spirituality is belonging. We are not our own people. Rather, we belong to each other. We belong to each other in the Church. And the Church belongs to God. Catholic spiritual life is communal life, through and through. We do not have one-on-one relationships with God. Christ is in our midst when we gather together, two or three of us, in His name. Our worship is communal rather than private. When we are judged, we are not judged on how well, as individuals, we kept the rules. We are judged on the love with which we did that. And so, we do pray, we do go to Church, we do observe moral precepts and regulations. But we do all of that in a communal way, not as isolated individuals. To be a Catholic is to belong.

It is to belong to other Catholics. It is to love our neighbor as ourselves.

Now, where can we find a better model of people belonging to each other than in a passionate couple? When two people are in love, they no longer have private, individual identities. They don't wake up in the morning thinking, "Well, now, what will I do today? I'll do this, and then I'll do that, and then I'll call Mary and see if we can get together for a while." No, when Joe's passion for Mary is burning, he wakes up thinking of her and of being with her, and plans his day accordingly. He is no longer a private self or individual. He is Mary's beloved, and that belonging to her constitutes his whole identity. When people talk about him to someone that doesn't know who he is, they will describe him. He is a handsome blond, works at such-and-such a store. But if that description doesn't work, there is one sentence that will identify him, unmistakably, every time: "He is Mary's boyfriend." That sets him apart from every other handsome blond man who works at the store. In fact, it sets him apart from everyone else in the whole wide world. His belonging to Mary identifies him, makes him be the person that he is.

And what about Mary's identity? Who is she? What can we say about her to identify her for someone who doesn't know who she is? Again, the answer is passion. How passionate is she for Joe? When she first fell in love with him, she belonged to him completely. She fell for him, hook, line, and sinker. And as long as that passion continued, she was his woman. She was no longer her own person. Every thought, every desire centered on Joe. She woke up in the morning thinking about him. She planned her days around their time together. It was unthinkable that she would make a move without considering him, informing him. Was her family planning a picnic for Sunday afternoon? Would Mary go along? That would depend. But certainly, when her desire for him and his enthusiasm for her were alive, it wouldn't occur to her to make plans according to her own wishes, and then wonder whether and how to fit Joe into them. And everyone else involved knew that. When Mama first announced the picnic, and cousin Bill asked if Mary would be there, what did she say? "That depends on Joe." It was well understood in the family that Mary's life now had a new center. If Joe had plans that took him away from Mary's family picnic, then it was assumed that Mary would miss the picnic too. She had a new identity. She belonged to Joe now, not to them.

Passionate belonging to each other, a belonging that is noticed and accepted by everybody else, is the heart and soul of the sacrament of matrimony. Our spiritual life begins with our baptism. And baptism is pre-eminently a sacrament of belonging. It is our initiation into the Church, not a private cleansing. We are now a member of that great assembly. We assume a new, communal ID. And that new identity is not an episodic event, forgotten once the ceremony is finished. It is a permanent, life-long, ongoing change in who we are. That new identity determines all the decisions we make thereafter. As members of the Church, we are no longer loners. We don't have our private opinions on religious matters anymore. Are we in a discussion about God, or life after death? Well, what we think on those matters is not what we choose and decide. It is what we think and decide together as a community of believers, the church. Likewise, are we debating with someone about some moral issue, such as abortion or nuclear war? How we think about these things is decided by our life in the Church. We don't have individual, private opinions. People who know that we are Catholics should be able to predict the stands that we will take just by knowing what stands our fellow Catholics have taken. They'll say, "Oh, you just think that way because you are a Catholic." But really, it's the other way around. I am a Catholic because I think that way. I am not a solitary individual trying to find my way through life all alone. I belong to a Church. And part of that belonging – a passionate, trusting belonging – is letting my fellow Catholics form my conscience. I don't have private moral opinions, following my own individual preferences. In my faith, and in my identity as a member of that believing community, in my belonging, I submit my conscience to the moral guidance of the community. We all belong to each other in the permanent, loving commitment that we made to each other at my baptism.

It is a fashion nowadays for some Catholics to pick and choose. Many do simply decide for themselves what stand they will take on abortion or divorce, or what they will believe about hell and divine mercy, or about the presence of Christ in the Eucharist. They will interpret the Bible according to their own private lights, too. And they will still call themselves Catholics. They even plead that they are following their individual consciences according to the teachings of Vatican II. But these people misunderstand the teaching on conscience. The basic decision that very individual conscience must make is the decision to belong to the Church.

Once that decision is made, the believer has a new, communal identity. He or she is not an individual with private opinions anymore. When someone takes that individualistic stance, then that person is giving up the communal identity of a baptized person. He or she is really stepping outside of the Church. To be private and independent is to resist belonging. And belonging is what Catholic spiritual life is all about. All of Catholic life is family life. It is life in the family of God.

But our belonging to the Church is not just a matter of beliefs. We don't just give our minds over to our fellow believers. The belonging which constitutes our newly baptized identities is passionate, enthusiastic, excited, unrestrained love for each other and for all human beings. Remember the Apostles on the first Pentecost? They were so excited about each other, and about the mission which they, as a group, had received from Christ, that people who saw them thought they were drunk. They were too excited to talk clearly. They couldn't be calm. They couldn't pass the sobriety test of walking a straight line on command. They were intoxicated with the message that they wanted to preach to the whole world. And that message was a message of belonging. "See how those Christians love one another." "By this will all men know that you are my disciples, that you love another." The love that the Apostles had for each other was a love of passionate belonging to each other. It was far beyond even that wonderful enthusiasm which the signers of our Declaration of Independence showed. They pledged to each other their lives, their fortunes and their sacred honor. Think of those men doing that! By putting their signatures on that piece of paper, they were taking the real risk of making themselves poor. They were risking a war that they might lose, and then they would spend the rest of their lives in public disgrace. They were even risking their very lives. And they cared enough about each other to take those risks together. What a bond was forged among them when they signed the Declaration of Independence! They truly belonged to each other in a passionate love.

And yet, that passionate, belonging love was pale in comparison to what the early members of the Church felt for each other. And their love, in turn, was pale in comparison to the love of Christ for His Church. Remember what he said at the Last Supper? "With desire have I desired to eat this Pasch with you." The love of God, the love that is poured forth in our hearts when we receive the Holy Spirit in baptism, is no dispassionate, on-again, off-again, dutiful acceptance of obligations. It is a passionate unifying love, a love that creates belonging. When God loves us, we belong to Him, and He to us. He is *our* God, and we are *His* people. (Notice those possessive pronouns.) And that belonging is no on-again, off-again affair, either. That is surely the message of the story of Hosea, and how he forgave his wife who was unfaithful to him. He took her back, because she was still *his*. Hosea and Gomer still belonged to each other and always would. The covenant by which God is *our* God, and we are *His* people, is just as constant. And so is our covenant with Christ, the new and everlasting covenant which He established at the Last Supper.

Now we can get some idea of how the sacrament of matrimony fits into the life of the Church. Sacramental couples are models, in their belonging to each other, of the total and constant belonging to each other which all Catholics are to have with all other Catholics. And that belonging within the Church is, in turn, a model for the belonging by which God is our God and we are His people. Sacramental couples show the rest of the world how to belong, how to love each other with passion, with enthusiasm, with excitement, with the selective vision that focusses on the beloved's goodness and does not turn off when faults come into view. That, my friends, is how all Christians ought to treat each other. And when we do, other people will notice how we love each other. And then, "they will know we are Christians by our love." Our love for each other will be a powerful magnet drawing other people into the same loving community. That's the modelling power of sexual passion!

The story of Hosea is a very powerful one. His wife abused him in the most serious way possible – through sexual infidelity. And that infidelity was a symbol of something even more serious – she abandoned their mutual belief in their God. She rejected the covenant that God had established with His people. Was there ever a better reason for a man to turn a woman out of his heart? Could any man have a better reason to let his passion for a woman cool? Could anyone be more powerfully tempted to put conditions on his love, to dole out his sexual favors as a reward for good behavior? Could any man have more justification for setting himself above his wife, adopting a critical, self-righteous air of superiority? He, if anyone, would be right to say, "How can we make love after something like that?" And yet, Hosea did none of these things. He did that very frightening thing that passion calls every husband and every wife to do: abandon his heart uncon-

ditionally and totally to the one he loved. Hosea belonged to her,
and he did not go back on that belonging. She belonged to him,
too. And that belonging was a permanent identity for both of
them. And so, when she asked his forgiveness and wanted to
return to his house and his bed, there was no question that he
would accept her. She belonged there. He took her back, passionately and unconditionally.

Belonging is the central feature of a sacramental marriage. And
belonging comes about in only one way – through passion. We
resist that total belonging, deep down in our hearts. I still find,
after nearly thirty years, that I often wake up in the morning with
a desire to plan "my" day. It is very hard to assume a new
identity, a coupled identity, and it takes a long time. But more
than time, it takes passion – passion that is deliberately cultivated
every single day, in every possible way. People who have not
experienced a long-lasting sexual relationship laugh at the idea that
sexual desire needs cultivation. They respond with shocked disbelief when we say that people who can have all the sexual
pleasure they want, whenever they want it, will shy away from it,
and find excuses to avoid it. And yet, ridiculous as it sounds, that
is precisely what happens. The cooling of passion in marriages is
not only due to the cultural myth which says that that's how it
should be. Cultural myths don't grow out of thin air. They have
roots in our minds and hearts. And the root of that particular
myth is a deep, inborn tendency toward intimacy-avoidance. We
shun passion because it leads us to belonging and to intimacy. And
belonging and intimacy mean giving up our precious individual
selves. There is nothing more frightening in human life. We resist
sexual desire, then, because we are afraid of intimacy. And we are
afraid of intimacy because it is a profound and total death to self.
And so, we are back to the Adam and Eve story. Those two
symbolic persons covered themselves physically, thereby putting
dampers on their sexual desire, out of shame. And shame – the
fear of psychological nakedness – is the symbol for the sinful self-
primacy that we need to be redeemed from.

Our redemption comes about in and through our sacramental
life in the Church. Shame and belonging – the two great opposites. Sin and grace – the same two opposites. Death and eternal
life – another phrase that says the same thing. Sexual restraint and
passionate self-abandon – the same pair in the perspective of the
sacrament of matrimony. I still remember when I first heard the
word "intimacy." It was in a conversation with a confessor who

had told me time and again, over a period of several years, that as a married person I was not supposed to copy the spirituality of celibates. My spiritual life was not in taking myself away from my husband to pray and read "spiritual books." (One evening I almost yelled at Ed for interrupting me when I was trying to read a new book about Christian charity!) No one had ever spoken to me about intimacy as a goal of the spiritual life. When this man did – he used the word almost casually, as if it were a category of thinking that was habitual with him – I felt a thrill deep inside me like I had never felt before.

That thrill was due, no doubt, to the fact that my confessor was advising me to do exactly what my own sexual desire was urging me to do. But I had never gotten that message before, that sexual desire is the basis of the spiritual life of married people. I was still going on the things I had heard in my early life – how sexual desire is a distraction from spiritual things. I was taught that being married is an obstacle to union with God. And so giving God my whole heart had to mean becoming a nun. I had a split in my mind between passion and spirituality, and as a result I gave myself only half-heartedly to both. After a long period of unlearning restraint and letting myself learn passion, that split has narrowed a lot. But it certainly hasn't disappeared. For example, I often wake up before Ed in the morning. I love to get up early and have an hour or so to myself at the beginning of the day. I like to think my own thoughts, enjoy the quiet house and the quiet street, and so on. And so, from time to time, I find myself getting out of bed very carefully so as not to wake Ed. Because if he wakes up, he might have loving on his mind. And then I might find I have it on my mind, too. And there go my plans for "my" early morning hours!

My mistake, of course, is in my self-image. I shouldn't even think of planning *my* day. But I still do. I'm one of those people who like to set up priorities every morning. "Here's the list of things I want to do today. And here's the order I'll do them in." If something unexpected happens so that I can't follow my plan, I feel a little tense and anxious, a little irritable, perhaps. But when I succumb to passion, everything is different. I wake up with a sense of awe at who I have turned out to be: this man's beloved, this man's lover. Everything in me relaxes, the day can develop as it will. I don't need an agenda because whatever happens, it's all passion. My anxious self-primacy is healed.

We do resist passion, then, incredible as that may seem to those who have not experienced that resistance. And we resist it precisely because it cements our belonging to each other. That belonging seems very nice when we first experience it. But as it deepens, it gets scary. We feel ourselves slipping away, out of our control. "Me first" doesn't really want to turn into "We first." Really, what we begin to feel is the fear of death. After all, why are we afraid to die? It's not just the pain, the separation from our loved ones, the regret of unfinished projects. These fears are important, of course, more so to some people than to others. But the deep-down, bottom line fear for all of us is the fear that we will no longer exist. We are afraid, even if we have some faith in life after death and our eventual resurrection, that if we give up, or lose, the self-identity that we have now, we will have nothing left. We fear that we will no longer exist as the selves that we've come to know and love. And it is that same fear, the fear of losing our very existence, that holds us back from the death to self that passion leads us into.

The lure of sexual pleasure gets us out of that fear when we fall in love. It also removes it when we make love, at least when we are properly aroused. But the ongoing passionate belonging of everyday life is something else. And that is what we need for the sacrament of matrimony. A sacramental couple would be one who modelled total, passionate abandon to each other in every detail of everyday life. They would be recognized in the Church as such a model. In fact, their wedding would be an ordination ceremony. It would be their official commissioning to "go forth and teach all nations" what it really means for Christians to love each other, to belong to each other. It would be the Church's public assurance that they do, indeed, have in them the Holy Spirit who is "the grace of God poured forth in our hearts." And so, in their passionate modelling of belonging, they would be a revelation, for all of the world, of Christ's love for His Church, the Church that belongs to Him and to which He belongs. And just as the Church is the sacrament of Christ, so is He the sacrament of God – a trinity in which three persons belong to each other in a passionate self-abandon that we can't even begin to imagine.

We see the importance of passion, then – the ongoing daily desire by which husband and wife experience their belonging to each other as a constant state of being. Passion is just as important in the life of a couple as prayer is in the life of a priest. In fact, passion is their prayer. It is their way of communing with the God whose love they wish to teach to the whole world. A truly holy priest does not look on his ordination ceremony as the end of a quest, an event over and done with, and now forgotten. Have you ever heard a priest say, "Ever since I was a little boy, I've wanted to have an ordination"? Wouldn't we laugh if we did hear that? No, what we hear is, "Ever since I was a little boy, I've wanted to *be* a priest." It's the being that counts. The ritual gets the being started. But it is the ongoing daily reality of being a priest, in every single moment of every single day, that counts as the sacrament of Holy Orders.

For couples, there is an exact parallel. Holy spouses don't say, or think.

"Well, now I've had the wedding I've always wanted. It's over and done with. And it was nice while it lasted. But now I'll just go on and live my life as if it hadn't happened. Oh, of course, we'll make love from time to time, and then the old excitement will come back for a while. But in between those times, I'm my own person. I have my life to live, my talents to develop, my interests to pursue. I'll have to make some sacrifices so we can live together peaceably. But mainly, I'm going to be the same person I was before."

Isn't that the mentality of a single person? And not even a baptized single person, but a pagan! No Christian has his or her "own" life to live. We are Christians by belonging to each other in ecstatic devotion. Isn't it obvious how that pagan, secular, single's mentality is a direct contradiction of the sacramental symbol? It doesn't signify belonging, but self-primacy. It is shame, not nakedness. It is sin rather than grace. Rather than revealing to the world the love of God for His people, it conceals that love. It is a direct countersign.

A sacramental couple, then, must be more than a man and woman who meet all the requirements for a valid marriage. They are not just a couple who, with proper sexual capabilities, made a free and willing permanent commitment to each other and the children who would be born to them. These are the conditions for any validly human marriage, for the human reality that can be transformed into a sacrament. But such a valid marriage can exist among pagans, without the transformation that would make it sacramental. In fact, we could even add passion – ongoing, constant passion – to that description, and still not have a sacramental couple. Passion is required, too, but even it is not enough. A sacramental couple have one important added feature: they are prophetic. They have accepted the call of the Church to cultivate the kind of passion that models the love of Christ for His

Church, and the love of God for His creation. Both of those loves are repeatedly called bridal, nuptial loves throughout the Bible, Old Testament and New. Sacramental couples are those who consciously accept that prophetic role in the Church.

But how, exactly, do they prophesy? In and through their sexual healing, and in being the kind of couple that the healing turns them into. Prophetic couples have some recognizable characteristics. For one thing, they know that they have a serious responsibility – a responsibility to the Church – to cultivate their passion. As they do that, they become transfigured people. They display a distinctive kind of spirituality. Their prayer, their service, their activities in the Church bear a special marital quality that is quite noticeable and that leads others to believe in the reality of love. The tenderized hearts that we mentioned earlier go out in a special way to everyone in the world. And the love that they send creates a special bond of belonging.

Even passion, then, is not a private affair. Some readers may get the impression that we are emphasizing sexual desire, and the cultivation of passion, too much. It might seem that we are encouraging couples to what the French call an *egoisme a deux* – a coupled selfishness. Won't those who practice Prime Time, who make their belonging to each other the focus of every waking moment, wind up neglecting their children? Won't they get so wrapped up in each other that they will not even notice other people? How will the world's work get done if its married couples are on a perpetual honeymoon? Children suffer when their parents give too much time and attention to each other, and too little to them. Where's the time and space for apostolic work? How can we be promoting romance when children are starving in Africa?

All we can say is that these objections would be based on a false understanding of the kind of sexual intimacy that we are proposing. The sexual healing that happens is an intimate marriage does not reinforce selfishness. It does not make us indifferent to the world. It heals the deep selfishness that all human beings need to be healed of. When that deep selfishness gets healed, it turns to a burning, passionate love for all of mankind. It becomes the desire with which Jesus desired to eat the Last Supper with his disciples. And we know, from His own words, what was on His mind at the Last Supper. It was the very meaning of His impending death. And He made that meaning clear in the prayer that He spoke at the Supper:

Father, may they all be one
As you, Father, are in me, and
I in you; I pray that they may be
one in us, that the world may believe
that you sent me. (JN 17, 21, The New American Bible).

Sexual healing, in other words, is apostolic. It is not isolating. It is part of the mission of the Church, which is to bring all men to unity with each other in love. And in that unity with each other, all will live in unity with God. But that unity does not come about through dispassionate good deeds. We sometimes hear that Jesus doesn't ask us to *like* our neighbors. He only asks us to love them. And love means doing good deeds, even without any feelings of enthusiasm. That's not what draws converts to the Church, though, at least not on any grand scale. Who likes to be treated that way? When it happens to us, we feel used rather than loved. We don't like it much when somebody is nice to us in order to score Brownie points with God.

But what happens to us inside when someone acts like they're crazy about us? How do we feel when someone is enthusiastic about being with us? How do we like it when someone likes us so much that they can't stay away, can't do enough for us, can't say enough good things about us and to us? We feel *loved* – that's how we feel. A passionate sexual partner certainly gives us that feeling. But true sexual healing, by spouses who are constantly passionate for each other, leads those spouses to love everyone that way. Love, when fired by sexual passion, spills over into all the other contacts that spouses have with other people. And that's the kind of love that makes the world go 'round. Dispassionate duty makes the world, and time, stand still. Passionate enthusiasm makes the world spin gloriously in its orbit.

But how does that unification come about? And how does sexual intimacy prophesy? It's not just by way of example, though that is important. Couples don't win people to the Church by saying, in effect, "See how we love each other!" They do so by saying, in word and deed, "See how we love you!" Sexual healing does not wall off two hearts from the rest of the world. It opens them up to the rest of the world. Obviously, when one of us falls in love, we open our heart and give its love to another person, someone outside our own little ego. And obviously, when a couple experience real sexual intimacy, their hearts also open up to welcome the children born to them. That would be wonderful enough, if that were all that happened. But there is so much more!

Sexually tenderized hearts are also opened up so that their love stretches even farther – to each other's family and friends, to all the people of their parish, to all Catholics, and, finally, to the whole world.

That stretching happened in a dramatic way to me and my husband. We adopted our two children in late middle age. We followed the Planned Parenthood motto: "Parenthood by choice, not by chance." But one big question that we faced, once we were qualified as adoptive parents, was whether or not to adopt a third child, and then a fourth, perhaps, or a fifth. Once we became aware of the numbers of children needing to be adopted, we wondered, quite seriously, where would we stop? Wherever that point was to be, it would be our choice that would select it. True, there is a severe shortage of adoptable healthy white infants, and people who want that kind of child have to go onto long waiting lists. But the situation is just the reverse with what are called "hard to place" children. They are the ones with physical handicaps, the mentally retarded, older children, biracial children, and so on. Anyone who wants to adopt one of those children will not have to go on a waiting list. Those children are on waiting lists, waiting for parents to take them into their hearts.

Since we were willing to take – and did take – children that are "hard to place," we were faced with the very real possibility of adopting more than our two. The agency told us, very clearly, that they would give us as many children as we would be willing to accept. We had to make a definite decision as to just how far our energy and our other resources could stretch. We decided, after lots of careful, prayerful, and passionate thought that two were all we could handle. We decided not to adopt any more children. But then we found out that our hearts could stretch much farther than what we thought. First of all, in our naivete, we thought that having two children meant loving, and caring for, two children! But as all parents soon learn, love does not end at the boundaries of a nuclear family. A large part of loving our own children is also loving their friends. And so, we often find five, six, or more children in our home, needing our love and care. And of course they do get that loving care, the loving care that we thought we couldn't give.

One day Ed startled me by the lengths that his love had reached, and stretched my love to match his. Our babysitter became pregnant, at the age of fifteen, and was determined to have an abortion. She came from a broken home, and wasn't getting the loving support she needed from her parents. I tried for several tearful hours one day to persuade her to give birth and let her baby be adopted. She finally ended the conversation by saying, "I'm sorry. I just couldn't carry a child for nine months, then give it away to strangers and wonder about it for the rest of my life." Later that day, I told my husband about the conversation, in deep despair at my failure to change Karen's mind. He said, without batting an eye, "Tell her we'll take the baby, and she won't have to wonder about it. She can be as close to it as she wants." I was aghast! Hadn't we decided that two were all we could handle? Hadn't I just finished three long, hard years to complete my schooling so that I could get the job that would educate our two? Wasn't Ed nearly sixty, for heaven's sake, and I in my late forties? What did he mean, "we'll take the baby"? All those thoughts raced through my mind in about ten seconds. When I caught my breath, I said, "Are you kidding?" He said, very quietly and matter-of-factly, "No, I'm not. If that's the only way to save that baby's life, then that's what we've got to do."

I went to sleep that night in great confusion and discouragement. I was really looking forward to my new job, and to the relative financial stability it would provide us. I had experienced – twice – the enormous amount of work involved, the sheer physical labor, in taking care of a new baby. And I really didn't know if I could go through all that again, especially with a baby that would not be mine. That baby might be taken away from me just about the time I really got attached to it. But by morning, I saw that Ed was right. After a long, passionate embrace and a good night's sleep, I felt the courage to take another baby into our hearts. And so, I called Karen with our offer.

As it turned out, Karen did change her mind about having an abortion. She carried her baby to term and gave birth. But instead of giving her baby to us, she kept her and, with a lot of help from her friends and family, is raising a lovely daughter, as a single parent.

But the point of the story is still valid. Passion had stretched our hearts. Our hearts had gone out to another child when we thought that they couldn't. And our passion also stretched Karen's heart, to love the child she once thought she had to destroy. Our hearts continue to grow, our love continues to expand, as our children gain more and more friends over the years. Please God, someday they will bring their beloved spouses-to-be to meet us, and then our hearts can stretch again. They will encircle whole families of in-laws, and their friends as well. And grandchildren, and their friends, perhaps even their spouses and in-laws, will feel the warmth of our passion. Our ability to love, which grows out of our passion for each other, has an endless ripple effect. For those we love find their ability to love strengthened, too, by the support that grows out of our passion. And as their love is strengthened, it is also stretched as their hearts open to an even wider circle of loved ones.

But something even deeper and more wonderful happens than that. What happens is what Jesus prayed for at the Last Supper: we who become one with each other also become one with Him, in His nuptial love for His Church. Our love doesn't just stretch out to our children, their friends, their future spouses and in-laws, and so on. Our hearts open up to every single person in the world, past, present and future. The idea of the Mystical Body of Christ begins to take on some reality for us. I remember very well how that opening of my own heart once took a real quantum leap. I had already been a philosophy teacher for several years when I fell in love and married. And I loved teaching. I felt that the classroom was "really me," where I really belonged. But about ten years later, I noticed that a real healing had taken place: I was able, for the first time in my life, to take a hard look at my motivation in my teaching. Under the guidance of a wonderful confessor, I had begun to be aware of the deep selfishness that lurks in every human heart, including my own. Without the support of the passionate love of Ed, I never would have had the courage to look at myself that honestly. When I did, I saw that a lot of my teaching was motivated by a search for my own security. That is, I enjoyed the classroom as much as I did because it gave me a chance to show off my knowledge. It also gave me a sense of success, a sense that there was, indeed, something that I could do successfully. It made me feel like I was somebody. I enjoyed feeling superior to my students.

But once I got the idea that my teaching ought to be motivated by love for my students, I experienced a deep and surprising change. In deciding what to teach, I would no longer design my courses around what I knew the best, or what I was interested in. I no longer looked at philosophy as a way of solving some of my own personal problems. Instead, I tried to see it from the point of view of the students whom I loved. What did they need to know for their lives? How was their stage of development different from mine? What would they be interested in? Which textbooks would be the most helpful to them? And gradually, as these questions took over my planning, I found my whole teaching focus transformed.

Before, I had taught mostly very abstract questions, those that could be answered by rigorous logical arguments. I spent a lot of time on such topics as proving the perfection of God, analyzing the connection between cause and effect, proving the immortality of the soul and the freedom of the will. The more abstract the topics were, the better I liked them. After the shift of my focus, I found myself going into whole new areas of philosophy, primarily those concerned with human relationships. Gradually, my interests changed. In trying to do what my students needed, I focussed more and more on the qualities of love, the meaning of sexuality, the dynamics of human relationships, marriage, family life, child-rearing, and so on. Of course, it's what I needed too. But I probably never would have looked at those questions without my desire for Ed and his desire for me.

The point is not that as sexual healing progresses, so does our interest in sex, love, and human relationships. That is probably true. But we are not suggesting that everyone become an academic specialist in these matters. The point of my own story is that sexual healing gives us a new power to love, no matter what our other profession might be, or even whether we have a profession. A woman who is a full-time homemaker will find the same stretching of her heart, if she dares to live in an aura of passion. The people she meets in the course of her day will be the people that she loves, with an enthusiasm and a joy that she never imagined she could find in herself. A man whose work is to prosecute criminals in a courtroom, or to audit the books of a corporation will find that he does so with a genuine love for the people he is connected with by his work. His job is not just a way of earning a living and enjoying the exercise of his talents. It is his way of acting out the love that builds the Church. It sounds crazy to say that a lawyer should love his clients, or a carpenter his customers, or a housewife her grocery clerks. But that is exactly the Christian craziness. That is the joy of heaven that begins on earth, if we let it.

The deepest sexual healing I have experienced has been this move away from a false, abstract intellectual life – one that was academic in the bad sense of the term – toward a more concrete involvement with real people. The change in my teaching focus brought a lot of other surprising changes along with it. For example, I had never liked history much, or been very interested in it. Poetry left me cold. So did art, and art history, and art criticism. I always loved to read, and did read a lot. But reading was an escape for me – a way of avoiding the people around me. I was afraid to love them, and afraid that they didn't love me, didn't even want to love me.

But one day, it hit me, as they say, like a ton of bricks – a new realization that has remained ever since. The assassination of President Kennedy triggered it, but it had been gestating in my depths for a long time. The realization was that all of us – all of us people, past, present and future – are in the same boat. We all have something very important in common: we need to live the best lives we can. We need to understand, and accept, and plunge into, the mystery of human love, especially as that love is threatened by death. We need to decide, to really *decide*, in the depths of our hearts, whether or not love is real. If it is not, then the atheistic existentialist philosopher, Albert Camus, is right: we should all commit suicide right now. But if it is, then we should bet our lives on it. We should try to be lovers, to everyone, with every fiber of our being, in every way we can, every day of our lives.

It struck me that that's what John F. Kennedy was trying to do in his political life, and in his marriage – to decide, in some deep and final way, about the reality of love. That's how politics originated, a long time ago. Men wouldn't even try to form governments if they were in total despair about the meaning of human life. They would, instead, commit suicide – or slowly die of boredom and apathy. Suddenly, I saw what poets and artists are trying to do, too. They, too, are trying to decide about the reality of human love. And so are the ordinary people I see on the bus, and in the supermarkets.

I had once studied the Roman poet whose most famous line was "Nothing human is foreign to me." Suddenly, those words meant something. That poet, and his poems, were no longer abstractions out of a book. History was not a dead past. I felt at one, in a very profound way, with every member of the human race. People in history – Jesus Christ among them – suddenly seemed real, and important, and part of the company of intimates that I belonged to. I even found myself praying to Plato one day, asking him to help me to understand his writings. They seemed terribly important to my daily life, and that of all the people I loved.

That realization, and sense of solidarity with all people everywhere, has been especially healing in regard to my deepest sorrow, my inability to bear children. Sterility came as a surprise to us, and as a devastating disappointment. I reached my personal low point one day when I knelt in the front pew of the church where we had been married, shook my fist at the tabernacle and said, "God damn you!" It doesn't make much sense to ask God to send Himself to hell, but that's how angry and confused I was!

I went on. "I do not care to spend my eternity as a sterile woman. So, if that's the salvation you've got in mind for me, you can keep it!" And I left the Church. I don't remember what I did the rest of that day. But the next morning, something very surprising happened. I had been in the habit of daily mass for many years, and when 8 a.m. rolled around again, I found I couldn't stay away. The lure of the Eucharist, which had always been strong, was still there! And yet, I had just told God to go to hell, and to take me along. What was happening?

What was happening was the sexual healing of the sacrament of matrimony. I did go to mass, feeling rather sheepish before the Good Shepherd. And I found myself able to begin to let go of the idea – which is a kind of self-worship – that I have anything to say about what my eternal salvation will be. That's entirely up to God, to the same God who gave us the Eucharist as His way of nourishing His own life in us. At first, I acted out of fear. I thought, "Hey – maybe an eternity of sterility is the only salvation available to me. I better take what I can get."

Gradually, though, over the years, that fear – the fear of being utterly lost if I let God do things His way – has evolved into a kind of loving trust in Him. The healing is by no means complete. But it has definitely begun. And it has, quite clearly, come about in and through my passion for Ed and his for me. It has been, and continues to be, a sexual healing. I remember thinking, for example, that I might have had children if I had married someone else. But I didn't want that. I didn't want just *Children* – I wanted Ed's children. And I certainly didn't want to be married to anyone else. I've known quite a few men to whom I was attracted sexually, whom I could imagine myself happily married to. But I've never wanted that for myself, even for a moment.

That's what I mean by sacramental belonging. I belong to Ed, and he to me, and that belonging gives us our identities. Some people find the very idea of belonging to someone repulsive. It sounds like being possessed and dominated, under someone's control and manipulation. It suggests that we won't be able to seek our happiness as we see fit. Probably all of us have something of that fear in us. We're like the 3-year-old boy when a visitor patted him on the head and said, "Whose little boy are you?" He drew himself up indignantly and said, "I'm nobody's. I'm myself." He was already feeling the power of that little punctuation mark, the apostrophe, which indicates the possessive form of a noun or pronoun.

But belonging, the kind of belonging that results from sexual healing, is something else. It's what we mean when we say that a picture should hang on a certain wall, for example: "It belongs right there! That's the right spot." That kind of belonging means, according to Webster, "to be related or connected with something or someone in a way that is right, or suitable." The belonging of passionate spouses is that kind. Our sexual healing does bind, or connect us, to each other. As passion continues, we come closer and closer, and a separation becomes more and more unthinkable. I know two different couples who have separated and then come back together more than once during their married lives. Passion binds them so tightly that they just don't know who they are when they are apart. Their identities are coupled identities.

But that belonging, and those coupled identities, are not just a form of emotional bondage. That belonging that we experience in our sexual healing is a deep, unmistakable sense that it is right, and fitting, and good that we should be together. It's the way things *ought* to be, somehow. When we try to picture ourselves not married, or not married to each other, it seems, somehow, just "not right." Any other arrangement just wouldn't be me.

I've experienced that sexual healing, too. It's something like an earlier identity-experience. When I was in college, I changed my major several times. I just didn't know what I wanted to be, how I wanted to spend my life. Even after I graduated (with a philosophy major), I didn't know. I was working as a waitress when the phone call came. A teacher in a local college had gotten sick in the middle of the year, and the president wondered if I would take over her classes. I had never even considered teaching philosophy as a possible career for myself. But I thought, "Why not give it a try? I don't know anything else I want to do." And so I accepted.

The very first class I taught was a thrill and a surprise, the first real identity-experience of my life. It gave me a dramatic sense of belonging. I kept thinking, "Wow! This is really it. This is me. This is where I belong." I *knew* that the philosophy classroom was right for me, it was where I ought to be. It was where I felt like myself.

But that identity-discovery was mild in comparison with what was to come – the marital belonging, and marital identity, that have come about in this wonderful sacrament of sexual healing. The healing is still in progress. It's not total yet. In fact, it's episodic, just as my passion is episodic. But when passion is intense – when I make a deliberate effort to keep it intense – I also have a deep and delicious feeling of belonging. I belong to Ed – I'm his wife, not my own person. And it's right, somehow. It's where I ought to be, where I fit in the best, where I am most myself. This, I feel, is the person God intended me to be. And I wouldn't have been able to be who I am in any other way. If I hadn't married, or had married someone else, or if I were to separate from Ed – none of that would be right. I just wouldn't be me. This is where I belong – in belonging to Ed.

In fact, I can notice a rhythm. Sometimes I don't have that deep, satisfying feeling that this is where I belong, that this is who I am. Some days, everything seems wrong. I can't teach or write or even think. I can't pray. I can't be affectionate with my children or my friends. Everything and everyone annoys me. I don't know who I am, or what to do, or how to be. The day passes with my trying one thing after another, and everything turning out wrong. I don't even like my favorite foods, my favorite clothes, my favorite music. I don't like myself.

And then, the whole syndrome reverses itself, and everything seems right again – comfortable, easy. I can teach and pray, be intimate with family and friends, enjoy just being, and being who I am. I feel like I'm right where I belong. For years, I didn't understand this rhythm, and had no control over it. But then one day I discovered the key: episodic belonging follows exactly the rhythm of episodic passion. When belonging fades, and identity gets clouded, there's a 90% chance – or more – that my passion has cooled. And so, the answer is obvious. The way to control that rhythm is to keep my passion alive. The way to discover my lost identity, to get back to where I belong, is to stimulate my desire for Ed. In the words of the theme song from *An Officer and A Gentleman*, "love lifts us up where we belong."

This cultivation of passion is, without a doubt, the key to marital spirituality. It is the heart and soul of the sexual healing which brings us to our salvation. How do we do it? Skin-to-Skin Prime Time is the Number 1 technique. But the other sacraments help, too. I seek out a priest who understands these matters. There are such priests around, here and there. And by the way, they are the ones who also understand celibacy, and live it in a credible, luminously sacramental way. When I find such a priest, I confess my sins – all the ways in which I have failed to be passionately desirous of Ed. Together, we read a Scripture passage that exhorts couples to passion. (There are more of these than we suspect, until we go looking for them.) Then my special priest devises a penance that will restore the passionate aura of our home. And I go and try to sin no more.

Over the years, this wonderful healing sacrament has taken a strange and wonderful turn. The pain of being sterile has been healed. The pain is still there. There is an emptiness in never having had children born to us. In fact, there is an awesome emptiness in the fact that persons who might have existed do not, and never will. Nothing can fill an emptiness like that. And yet, it is due to that emptiness, that sterility, that we have experienced a fertility that we couldn't have experienced in any other way.

I am referring, first of all, to the two adopted children that we have taken into our hearts. Thanks to our adopting them, they belong to us, and we to them, in a way that would not have been possible if we had had children born to us. They are as truly the offspring of our passion as if they were born to us, and find their identities, their belonging, in its aura. This is where they belong, too. They are not just connected to us – they are who they are because of it. And that connection is right, just exactly right. They are right where they ought to be. And that is true of the continuing pain of their not being with their biological parents.

But my own healing is the one I understand the best. And that has been deep and surprising. In the early days of my bitterness about being a sterile woman, I was thoroughly self-centered and self-pitying. Whenever I saw a pregnant woman, or heard of someone giving birth, I would get angry at God and down on myself. Why did He do this to me? Why did He think she was so much better than I, so much more worthy of the awesome gift of a child? I couldn't even offer sympathy to a dear friend when she had a miscarriage. I would have been delighted to have a miscarriage!

But gradually, even those feelings have changed. Now, on my good days – my passionate days – I feel happy about every pregnant woman I see. I want to hold, and bond with, every new baby that I meet. It just seems good, and right, that more and more people should be born, to experience this wonderful mystery of life and love. The words of one of my friends come back to me, with new meaning every time: "Marriage isn't for children. Children are for marriage." We don't marry in order to have children. We marry for the sake of each other's sexual healing, to be instruments of each other's salvation. And we have (or adopt) children, and raise them in the aura of our own passion, in the hope that they, too, will someday experience that same sexual healing.

Sexual healing, then, is something much deeper than what the recently popular song referred to. It doesn't just make us feel good. It does do that, sometimes, but it brings a lot of pain, too. Sexual healing leads us to forgive. It's not just that we excuse each other's faults, and overlook a thousand little hurts. Sexual healing leads to really deep forgiveness. It has led me, gradually – though not yet completely – to forgive God for having His own ideas about how my life should go. I no longer feel hurt and angry, worthless and insecure, because of my inability to bear children. I feel a certain sense that it is right, somehow, that I didn't. It is right to be exactly who I am, and where I am, to have the children I have and the husband I have, and no others.

When I am passionate, and enjoy the deep sense of being right where I belong, I find a surprising tenderness in myself. On my passionate days, I don't have to pray for patience, or strive for it by taking deep breaths and counting to 10. I have something better than patience. I have insight, realization, awareness. I can see, to some extent, how the world looks to other people, how their view makes sense to them, even though it is different from mine.

One day, a neighbor boy came to interview our family for a high school report. "Eddie," he asked our 10-year-old son, "how does it feel to be adopted?" I expected Eddie to say what I would have said – that it is wonderful, that we have a warm and happy family life. But he didn't. He didn't see it that way. What he said was, "Well, it's all right. At least it's better than being abortioned. If I was abortioned, I wouldn't be here at all." The poignancy of a child feeling relief at not having been murdered often comes back to me. And it reminds me that the people who annoy and irritate me might be looking at the world from a different viewpoint than mine. I'm not the most compassionate person in the world. But I'm certainly better than I would have been without the tender passion I've experienced over the years.

When I get such glimpses of what sexual healing can be, the Eucharist takes on a whole new dimension. Recently I opened the

Sunday missal, just at random, to see if anything in the mass spoke of passion and sexual healing. I was almost overwhelmed by what I found. The mass was for August 18, 1985, the Twentieth Sunday in Ordinary Time, in the "B" cycle. The entrance song caught my eye at once, a psalm verse (PS 18, vs. 10–11) that describes sexual healing better than I could ever do:

> God, our protector, keep us in mind;
> Always give strength to your people.
> For if we can be with you even one day,
> It is better than a thousand without you.

As passionate spouses, we protect each other, keep each other in mind, and give each other strength. Thus is our sexual healing an image, a faint but real reflection of the love with which God loves his people. And though our healing is not yet perfect, though our passion is still episodic, yet we do have it from time to time. And one day with passion, since it is a day with God, is better than a thousand days without either one.

The first prayer of the day's mass seemed to be designed for couples, too:

> God, our Father, may we love you in all things and above all things, and reach the joy you have prepared for us beyond all imagining.

We think we've found that joy when we first fall in love. And we have, in a way. Early passion leads to a belonging that is, in a way, total. And yet, what is total can grow. The new and deeper healing that comes with years of passion is, indeed, beyond all our imagining. Remember the group I mentioned earlier, who invited me to speak to them about marital spirituality? That was the meeting at which Fran, a widow for 7 years, spoke of the new intimacy that she and Don had found as he lay dying in a crowded hospital room. Fran was older than me, by 15, perhaps 20 years. Several other couples in that group were about her age, too. I found my encounter with those couples to be a deeply healing experience. In my youthful, and even in my middle-aged, naivete, I had a kind of prejudice against old people that I had scarcely been aware of. "What do they know about passion and romance?" I used to think. "Those things are long gone for them." But the conversation that evening showed me how wrong I was. If we want to see really lusty passion, strong devotion, and the profound sexual healing that sacramental mariages bring, we should look to old couples. For they have that healing, and that feeling, more deeply than the rest of us.

The evening with that group of old people did not just heal some of my prejudice against and contempt for them. It also made me less afraid of getting old myself, and even of dying. Now I see that passion keeps growing, that the joys of sexual intimacy in old age can be far beyond what we feel in earlier life. The ability to express desire and passion declines with age. The muscles we use for hugs and caresses, for smiles and winks, for tender looks and gestures, get weak and atrophy. But the fire of passion is still there, more deeply healing than ever before.

As I continued to read the mass for August 18, 1985, I began to wonder if it was originally written as a wedding mass. The first reading was *Proverbs 9, 1–6*, which spoke of Wisdom preparing her banquet, and inviting ordinary people from the city to come and partake of her food and wine, and give up lives of foolishness. Don't those words speak to all of who, as ordinary human beings, have what it takes to keep our passion alive? Truly, it is the way of foolishness to live in restrained, dutiful benevolence toward each other. We'll never be healed that way, for dispassionate, controlled kindness is really a way of keeping ourselves to ourselves. The way to fuller life, the life that Wisdom offers, is the wholehearted abandoning of ourselves to each other in passion. That is what stretches our hearts and heals the fears that keep us huddled to ourselves.

St. Paul's words to the Ephesians, Chapter 5, verses 15–20 were our second reading. Paul tells us to watch our conduct, to act like wise people rather than fools. He tells us to discern the will of the Lord, to be filled with the Spirit, to live with constant praise and gratitude in our hearts. It would be hard to find a better description of a passionate couple. For us married people, the will of the Lord, the way to act wisely, is the way of sexual healing. When we keep our passion alive, we are filled with the Spirit. Our hearts are grateful and full of praise. We worship, in awe, the God who draws us into the mystery of His Love.

The gospel for the day was one of the great Eucharistic readings (JN 6, 51–58), in which the Jews quarreled about the meaning of Jesus' promise to give us His flesh to eat, so that we might never die. Jesus simply repeated that His flesh is real food, His blood real drink, and that this food and drink truly do nourish the divine life that He gives us. This gospel reading clearly speaks to the close relationship between the two great sacraments, Eucharist and Matrimony. The Eucharistic Banquet, like Wisdom's banquet described in *Proverbs*, gives the food and drink which nourish a couple's life of passionate abandon and sexual healing. Thus does the Eucharist strengthen and protect a sacramental marriage.

But the strengthening goes the other way, too. The Eucharist is the high point of Christ's enactment of His nuptial love for His Bride, the Church. It is the time of His making all men one, as He and the Father are one. But the success of each mass in doing that depends on the fervor of the people who take part in it. The mass, too, is a sacrament. It is a sign or symbol that has to be accurate in order to effectively cause what it symbolizes. And so, couples have a lot to do with whether a mass is effective or not for building up the unity of the Church. Do we bring our passionate desire to the mass, or do we keep it under wraps, or even leave it at home behind closed bedroom doors? We owe it to the Church to bring it to the altar, and to take it back again, nourished and refreshed, intoxicated, even. When we approach the altar with passion cooled or dormant, we are like the man who comes to the altar with something against his brother. Like him, we should be reconciled first, renewing our passion, and then offer the gift of that passion at the altar.

In fact, the Offertory prayer for August 18, 1985, speaks clearly and eloquently of how we ought to do this very thing:

> Lord, accept our sacrifice as a holy exchange of gifts. By offering what you have given us, may we receive the gift of yourself.

Our passion is what God has given us. It is, in fact, His own life in us. When we give it to Him as our Eucharistic offering, we receive it back again in Communion. The Eucharist is the marital act *par excellence.*

The communion song for August 18, 1985 repeats a verse of the gospel, so as to reinforce it:

> I am the living bread from Heaven, says the Lord;
> if anyone eats this bread, he will live forever.

One of my friends, a deeply devout Jesuit priest, heard those words at a funeral once, and exclaimed, "By God, if you can believe that, you can believe anything." We often don't realize what astounding things Jesus asks His followers to believe. Life after death? Are you kidding? Eating living bread, which gives us eternal life? If we eat this, we will never die? Is He serious, or what?

And yet, we can find the courage to believe such nearly incredible things. Most of us find that courage in the sexual healing that we experience in the sacrament of matrimony, when we *know*, in our hearts and bones, our muscles and nerves, that love is, indeed, real; then we can believe that God, the most real being of all, is Love. And once we believe that, we can, in the words of my Jesuit friend, "believe anything." We cannot just believe – we can take part. We can come to Widsom's banquet, give up our foolish lives, and eat the living bread. And then we can receive what we pray for in the Postcommunion Prayer for August 18, 1985:

> God of mercy, by this sacrament you make us one with Christ. By becoming more like Him on earth, may we come to share His glory in Heaven, where He lives and reigns for ever and ever.
>
> Amen

What does it mean for couples to "become more like Him on earth"? It means to love with passionate abandon, first each other, and then our children, and then all the world. It means to say "Nothing human is foreign to me." It means to open up our family to the world, to stretch our hearts to every member of the People of God.

One day as we were leaving for the last mass on a Sunday morning, Eddie, age 5, suddenly balked and announced that he wasn't going to go. "I'm not going," he said. "I don't care if you ground me for the rest of my life. It's stupid, and it's boring, and it's too long, and I'm not going to go." There's been a lot of talk, and a little bit of action, in the last 20 years towards reforming the liturgy. But we still have much to do. One way to let people see that the Mass is meaningful and relevant to their lives is to connect it with the passion of sacramental couples. Marital passion and liturgy should feed each other. Too often, we look askance at couples showing any signs of affection toward each other during the mass. And yet, when is a more appropriate time for a passionate, tender, eager embrace than at the Kiss of Peace? What we should look askance at is couples who give each other the same brief, impersonal handshake they give to everyone else.

Making passionate couples more prominent in the Church, then, would be a powerful liturgical reform. In fact, it would make the Mass less 'stupid, boring, and too long" even for children. When our children see how Prime Time builds our passion, and tenderizes our hearts toward them, they can hardly wait to close the door behind us. If the Sunday Mass became just as effective – an obvious instrument of sexual healing – they would be just as eager to lead us to the altar.

In fact, sexual healing in the sacrament of matrimony will support the Church's social justice mission in a special way, too. Take the simple matter of paying taxes to support our welfare system. Is that just an onerous burden that our laws impose on us? Is it a way in which a faceless government takes our money away from us and gives it to freeloaders? Or is it an opportunity for us to act out the love for all human beings, and especially for all children, that passion urges us to? It's hard, once our shell is cracked, to love one child without loving all. And most of the people on welfare are children – children whose parents, for one reason or another, are not taking care of them. The nuclear issue is another area of concern that is transformed by the passion of intimate couples. In fact, any social justice issue that we can name is important for those of us who experience ongoing sexual healing in our marriages. For issues are not really issues – they are people. Political decisions affect the lives of our fellow members of the Mystical Body. As we love people more and more, we care more and more about those political decisions. Do we care about protecting our environment? If we care about the lives, the health, the comfort and the recreation of our beloved fellow members of the Mystical Body, yes, we do. Passionate spouses follow the motto of the Roman poet, "Nothing human is foreign to me." We say, "Nothing concerned with love for any human being is foreign to me."

As we act our passionate belonging to everyone – first to our fellow baptized Catholics, and then to everyone else – the people we love will notice something. They will begin to believe in the reality of human love and human belonging. They will believe because they will see these realities before their very eyes. And so, the tenderized hearts of passionate spouses do much more than set an example, or give a model, of how all people ought to belong to each other in love. Those hearts actually take people into them, widening the circle of love like ripples from a rock thrown into a lake. People who experience being loved by passionate couples will, sooner or later, ask themselves the all-important question, "Is this for real? Are these people for real? Dare I believe that love is real, and not just a fantasy?" And then, as they see the answer to those questions answered, in the flesh, before their very eyes, it will be easy for them to take the next step. They will be empowered to stake their lives on that sentence in John's First Epistle, which puts all of Catholic belief, and all of Catholic life, into a few brief words:

> God is Love,
> And he who abides in love,
> Abides in God,
> And God in Him. (I John, 4:16, *The New American Bible*).

QUESTIONS TO DISCUSS TOGETHER AS A COUPLE

1. Name some ways in which your own sexual healing has tenderized your heart.
2. Discuss the prayers and readings from last Sunday's Mass in terms of sexual healing.
3. Describe some experiences which have given you a clear sense of belonging. Contrast those with experiences which made you feel that you didn't belong.
4. What can we learn, from our experience of marital passion, about Christ's love for the Church?
5. What can we learn about marital passion from Christ's love of the Church?
6. How does sexual healing lead us to a concern for social justice?